Y0-EEL-306

Creating Digital Video in Your School:

How to Shoot, Edit, Produce, Distribute, and Incorporate Digital Media into the Curriculum

Ann Bell

Linworth Books

Professional Development Resources for
K-12 Library Media and Technology Specialists

Library of Congress Cataloging-in-Publication Data

Bell, Ann, 1945-
  Creating digital video in your school / Ann Bell.
      p. cm.
  Includes bibliographical references and index.
   ISBN 1-58683-186-0 (pbk.)
  1. Digital video. 2. Instructional materials centers. 3. Multimedia
library services. 4. High school libraries. I. Title.
TK6680.5.B45 2005
006.6'96--dc22

                                    2004030202

Published by Linworth Publishing, Inc.
480 East Wilson Bridge Road, Suite L
Worthington, Ohio 43085

Copyright © 2005 by Linworth Publishing, Inc.

All rights reserved. Purchasing this book entitles a librarian to reproduce activity sheets for use in the library with-in a school or entitles a teacher to reproduce activity sheets for single classroom use within a school. Other por-tions of the book (up to 15 pages) may be copied for staff development purposes within a single school. Standard citation information should appear on each page. The reproduction of any part of this book for an entire school or school system or for commercial use is strictly prohibited. No part of this book may be electronically reproduced, transmitted, or recorded without written permission from the publisher.

ISBN: 1-58683-186-0

5 4 3 2 1

Table of Contents ———————————————————

Table of Figures

About the Author

Ann Bell is the high school media specialist at Camanche High School, Camanche, Iowa. Before coming to Camanche in 1996, Ann was a media specialist in Montana, Oregon, and Guam. Ann received her B.A. degree from the University of Northern Iowa, a library media endorsement from the University of Montana, and a Master of Library and Information Studies from the University of Hawaii. She has completed postgraduate work at Drake University and the University of Northern Iowa.

Ann received the 2001 Informational Technology Pathfinder Award from the American Association of School Librarians and the Follett Software Company, was featured in the December 2001 issue of *Teacher/Librarian,* and was the recipient of the 2002 Iowa Educational Media Association Lamplighter Award.

Ann has published a series of eight books for Heartsong Presents Book Club. Barbour Publishing combined the first four books into *Montana,* which was on the Christian Booksellers' Association Bestseller List in 2000. *Montana Skies,* the combined last four books, was published in May 2002. The novel, *Mended Wheels,* was released in July 2002.

Aknowledgments

I would like to thank Joan Vandervelde, Online Professional Development Coordinator for the University of Wisconsin–Stout, for her encouragement and support in developing the online class *Creating Computer Video for the Classroom and School* that has been offered through the University of Northern Iowa and the University of Wisconsin–Stout, which led to this book. Without her support in providing quality professional development online and her support of educational technology, this book would not have happened.

Introduction

Educators would never consider teaching children to read but not to write, since both are essential for effective communication. Today educators are recognizing that communications in the world of their students are primarily through media and technology and that they must teach students not just to "read" electronic media, but also to create it. Therefore, it is critical that student media production become a routine, integrated part of the curriculum and not left as an extra-curricular activity.

In the last 10 years, multiple intelligences, the impact of visual literacy, the emphasis on standardized testing, and the rush of new technologies have challenged library media specialists and other educators as never before. As I faced these demands within my own school, along with a shrinking budget available for hardware and software, it became apparent that there was a lack of professional resources for the video novice.

To help meet that need I searched the Internet and plowed through numerous books and professional journals in order to broaden my understanding of the mechanics of digital video editing and the value of digital video within the school curriculum. With that information I developed an online professional development course *Creating Computer Video for the Classroom* for the University of Northern Iowa. Two years later the entire professional development program transferred to the University of Wisconsin—Stout.

While teaching professional development classes of busy professionals, I recognized the need for a concise reference book that educators could read from beginning to end or use as a reference book for specific video questions and problems.

This book is written in a straightforward style to appeal to busy educators who are novice video producers. It provides insight on how to use digital video to enhance the curriculum as it helps educators meet state and national standards in technology and the content areas.

To assist in the preparation of digital videos this book provides guidance in the selection of hardware and software, preparation of pre-production checklists and storyboards, elements of video editing, methods of final distribution, organization of a school broadcast center, criteria for evaluating student work, and tips on preparing school news shows.

As informational technology exploded around them, library media specialists, teachers, and administrators discovered they would need to use computers regularly to meet realistic educational goals to prepare students adequately for 21st century skills. Because technology tools were constantly changing and learning resources varied among the different learning environments, a need for consistent standards became apparent if students were to meet their fullest potential in becoming lifelong learners in an information age.

The International Society of Technology in Education (ISTE) has taken a leadership role in establishing standards for students, teachers, and administrators for the effective use of information technology in education. In order for teachers to be better prepared to assist their students in achieving the student technology standards, educators must also be well versed in the potential and use of the technology themselves.

Based on the *ISTE National Educational Technology Standards (NETS) and Performance Indicators for Teachers* <http://cnets.iste.org/teachers/pdf/page09.pdf> topics covered in this book will help teachers meet the following ISTE-T Standards:

"Standard I -Technology Operations and Concepts"

"Performance Indicator A: demonstrate introductory knowledge, skills, and understanding of concepts related to technology."

For example: The library media specialist and teacher are able to select the appropriate video-editing hardware and software, videotape a clip, edit, and output that clip to a usable format.

"Standard II — Planning and Designing Learning Environments and Experiences"

"Performance Indicator A: design developmentally appropriate learning opportunities that apply technology-enhanced instructional strategies to support the diverse needs of learners."

For example: A teacher assists her eighth grade students with limited reading skills in preparing video books for the primary grades. The students videotape their classmates reading stories of interest to lower elementary students, edit the video, and present it to the kindergarten class.

"Performance Indicator C: identify and locate technology resources and evaluate them for accuracy and suitability."

For example: The library media specialist or teacher is familiar with several quality Web sites that evaluate digital video hardware and software and is able to compare the features of a specific product with the industry standard.

"Standard III — Teaching, Learning, and the Curriculum"

"Performance Indicator B: use technology to support learner-centered strategies that address the diverse needs of students."

For example: A library media specialist can prepare a video that explains how to locate an item in the online catalog. If a student forgets, he can access an online tutorial before asking for assistance.

"Performance Indicator C: apply technology to develop students' higher order skills and creativity."

For example: The 10th-grade history teacher helps a group of students create a video on life in the 1860s. Certain items or customs that were not available or done during that period are intentionally inserted into the video. Classmates will view the videotape, try to find what is out of place, and explain why it should not have been included in the scene.

"Performance Indicator D: manage student-learning activities in a technology-enhanced environment."

For example: A high school teacher helps students build electronic portfolios using digital video.

"Standard V — Productivity and Professional Practice"

"Performance Indicator A: use technology resources to engage in ongoing professional development and lifelong learning."

For example: A library media specialist or teacher can capture and store digital video clips on teaching strategies that will assist them in their educational environment.

"Performance Indicator C: apply technology to increase productivity."

For example: An art teacher videotapes a lesson on how to throw a pot on the potter's wheel and if students are absent during the presentation, she merely refers them to the video and does not have to take valuable class time to reteach the lesson.

"Performance Indicator D: use technology to communicate and collaborate with peers, parents, and the larger community in order to nurture student learning."

For example: The library media specialist videotapes and edits a class working in an overcrowded computer lab and presents it to the school board with a proposal to purchase a quantity of handheld computers to inexpensively alleviate the overcrowded lab.

"Standard VI — Social, Ethical, Legal, and Human Issues"

"Performance Indicator A: model and teach legal and ethical practice related to technology use."

For example: A social studies teacher assists her students in obtaining copyright permission for a patriotic song they want to use as a background to their mock election commercial.

"Performance Indicator B: apply technology resources to enable and empower learners with diverse backgrounds, characteristics, and abilities."

For example: A middle school teacher produces a school news show and rotates student assignments so each student learns the skills involved in each position.

"Performance Indicator C: identify and use technology resources that affirm diversity."

For example: A middle school teacher assists her students in videotaping and editing video clips taken at the heritage day celebration where students presented a custom that was unique to their heritage.

"Performance Indicator D: promote safe and healthy use of technology resources."

For example: A library media specialist teaches students the correct way to use the video equipment before it is checked out of the media center.

"Performance Indicator E: facilitate equitable access to technology resources for all students."

For example: The seventh grade teacher makes sure every student in the group has a turn in using the video camera so usage of the technology is not limited to one student.

With the help of this book, library media specialists and teachers will gain a fresh perspective of a technology skill that can be used to fulfill a multitude of educational standards in both the technology and the content area fields. As educators personally master video-editing skills and understand the value of visual literacy in the classroom, their students will be better prepared for the 21st century skills of digital-age literacy, inventive thinking, effective communication, and high productivity.

Meeting content area standards with video need not be limited to the educators' skills or creativity. The right tools, in the right students' hands, at the right time can open an entire area of visual literacy and lead to higher-order thinking skills and enrichment in students' lives that will stay with them for the rest of their lives.

Reprinted with permission from *National Education Technology Standards for Students: Connecting Curriculum and Technology,* copyright © 2000, ISTE (International Society for Technology in Education), 800.336.5191 (U.S. & Canada) or 541.302.3777 (International), <www.iste.org, iste@iste.org>. All rights reserved. Permission does not constitute an endorsement by ISTE.

Chapter 1

Visual Literacy in Education

Impact of Media on Student Learning

Since the beginnings of human culture, visual awareness has been a key element in communication. The symbols of early cave paintings held a deep significance for the artists and cultures that produced them. Today a visually literate person is able to discriminate and interpret the visual actions, objects, and symbols he encounters in the environment around him. Through the creative use of these visual competencies, a person is able to communicate more effectively with others.

The 21st century incorporates the print-defined literacy of the past with an instantaneous flood of sounds and symbols along with the assembly of text, data, photos, and their magical collage. Library media specialists and other educators must help students develop new intellectual skills or perceptions in order to master the flood of symbolic and audio representations that surround them.

Library media specialists and teachers continually search for ways to best prepare young people for success in the 21st century. To help meet this need, the Partnership for 21st Century Skills provides a compelling vision and an urgent call for action in its "Mile Guide for 21st Century Skills," at <www.21stcenturyskills.org/downloads/P21_Report.pdf>.

Page four of the executive summary of their Letter to America's Education Leaders from the Board of Partnerships for 21st Century Skills challenges:

"Today's education system faces irrelevance unless we bridge the gap between how students live and how they learn. Schools are struggling to keep pace with the astonishing rate of change in students' lives outside of school. Students will spend their adult lives in a multitasking multifaceted, technology-driven, diverse, vibrant world—and they must arrive equipped to do so. We also must commit to ensuring that all students have equal access to this new technological world, regardless of their economic background."

For over 25 years the Center for Media Literacy (CML), <www.medialit.org/>, has provided clear and concise interpretation and articulation of the theory and issues in media literacy. In their "MediaLit Kit: Teacher's/Leader's Orientation Guide", <www.medialit.org/pdf/mlk_orientationguide.pdf>, the Center for Media Literacy provides guidance to library media specialists and other educators on how to best help students incorporate media into their learning environment. In evaluating media, the CML poses five questions viewers should consider when viewing or listening to all types of media.

Media Literacy: Five Key Questions

1. Who created this message?

2. What techniques are used to attract my attention?

3. How might different people understand this message differently from me?

4. What lifestyles, values, and points of view are represented in or omitted from this message?

5. Why was this message sent?

<www.medialit.org/reading_room/pdf/04KeyQuestionsBW.pdf >

Faced with the intensity and vast array of media stimuli, library media specialists and other educators are being forced to the forefront to further the understanding of visual literacy and apply media literacy and media production to all levels of the curriculum using digital technology. By producing media themselves, students obtain a deeper understanding of how varying light, color, movement, and sound can influence a message and sometimes change it completely.

Parents, administrators, and teachers often lament over their students' fascination with mass media on television, the Internet, and video games, and assume that these gaudy baubles steal attention from the matters of substance they hope to impart. While there may be some truth to media distraction, educators might be competing with a medium that has a clearer framework of presentation than the traditional classroom setting.

From the beginning, actors on stage and television were taught techniques to engage an audience and took for granted that their audience was vulnerable to distractions and preconceptions that got in the way of the communication process. If educators are to reach the students of the 21st century, they may need to utilize some of the same techniques as the popular media of the day.

Communication Skills in Video Production

Words and pictures are collections of symbolic images. Words are signs composed of lines, curves, and open and closed shapes while pictures can be presented in a variety of colors, forms, depths, and movements. Visual learning is the process of learning from pictures and media and includes the construction of knowledge by the learner because of seeing the visual image.

The International Visual Literacy Association (IVLA) <http://www.ivla.org/org_what_vis_lit.htm> best explains visual literacy. The term "visual literacy" was first coined in 1969 by John Debes, one of the most important figures in the history of IVLA. Debes offered (1969b, 27) the following definition of the term:

"Visual Literacy refers to a group of vision-competencies a human being can develop by seeing and at the same time having and integrating other sensory experiences. The development of these competencies is fundamental to normal human learning. When developed, they enable a visually literate person to discriminate and interpret the visible actions, objects, symbols, natural or man-made, that he encounters in his environment. Through the creative use of these competencies, he is able to communicate with others. Through the appreciative use of these competencies, he is able to comprehend and enjoy the master-works of visual communication."

Copyright © The International Visual Literacy Association

Visual literacy deals with what can be seen and how we interpret what is seen. It includes the study of the physical processes involved in visual perception, the use of technology to represent visual imagery, and the development of intellectual strategies to interpret and understand what is seen.

Visual communication consists of using pictures, graphics, and other images to express ideas and to teach people. For visual communication to be effective, the receiver must be able to construct meaning from seeing the visual image.

Creating videos provides students with practice in critical 21st century communications skills. One of the biggest challenges in visual literacy is to accurately turn the written or spoken word into a visual context. The video production process involves critical-thinking, general observation, analysis, and perspective-making skills. As students produce their own videos, they will look at visual imagery as a series of choices made by writers, directors, actors, editors, and will consider how visual images differ in their ability to communicate ideas and emotions to an audience.

Components of visual literacy require knowledge of the history, properties, and characteristics of light and how it is used to influence moods and feelings. Visual literacy involves an understanding of the four visual cues that the brain is physically designed to notice: color, form, depth, and movement.

While watching a professionally produced video, older students may become suspicious of attempts to be persuaded or manipulated. By producing their own video, students will be able to use similar tools and experience first hand how the use of media can manipulate the emotions of others, influence their thinking, inspire and define the culture, and dictate fashion.

The North Central Regional Educational Laboratory best described the value of media production and visual literacy when they wrote in *enGauge 21st Century Skills—Visual Literacy* <www.ncrel.org/engauge/skills/vislit.htm>.

"Students Who Are Visually Literate:

Have Working Knowledge of Visuals Produced or Displayed through Electronic Media

- Understand basic elements of visual design, technique, and media.
- Are aware of emotional, psychological, physiological, and cognitive influences in perceptions of visuals.
- Comprehend representational, explanatory, abstract, and symbolic images.

Apply Knowledge of Visuals in Electronic Media

- Are informed viewers, critics, and consumers of visual information.
- Are knowledgeable designers, composers, and producers of visual information.
- Are effective visual communicators.

- Are expressive, innovative visual thinkers and successful problem solvers."

"Copyright © (2004) North Central Regional Educational Laboratory, a wholly owned subsidary of Learning Point Associates. All rights reserved. Reprinted with permission."

Applying Student-Produced Digital Video to NET Standards

Since the 1970s, educators have realized that technology had a tremendous impact on student learning. Its potential for use appeared endless, but there were varying degrees of beneficial results in the use of educational technology. As soon as the first computers began arriving in schools, it became obvious that computer-related technology must become a tool rather than a toy. As informational technology exploded around them, library media specialists, teachers, and administrators realized they would need to use computers regularly to meet realistic educational goals to prepare students adequately for adult citizenship in the Information Age. Since technology tools were constantly changing and learning resources varied among the different learning environments, the need for consistent standards became apparent if students were to meet their fullest potential and become lifelong learners.

The International Society of Technology in Education (ISTE) has taken a leadership role in establishing standards for students, teachers, and administrators as to the effective use of information technology in education. In order for teachers to be better prepared to assist their students in achieving the student technology standards, educators must also be well versed in the potential and use of the technology themselves.

ISTE National Educational Technology Standards (NETS) for Students

<http://cnets.iste.org/students/s_stands.html>

Teachers who use digital videos to achieve the NET Standards for Teachers will also pass that knowledge on to their students who will master the following NET Standards for Students when using digital videos.

"Standard I—Basic Operations and Concepts"

"Students demonstrate a sound understanding of the nature and operation of technology systems."

Example: While preparing a video of their science experiments, 10th grade students learned the nature and operation of pre-production, production, and post-production of the video system along with the basic elements involved in each step.

"Students are proficient in the use of technology."

Example: As seventh graders in an exploratory class received instruction on the features of a video camera, and then videotaped a short clip on 'Life in My School' they become proficient at the basic use of a video camera.

"Standard II—Social, Ethical, and Human Issues"

"Students understand the ethical, cultural, and societal issues related to technology."

Example: Students in the high school television production class became aware of the ethical, cultural, and society issues involved in videotaping their news production on location when they obtained permission from the local police department and the local business owner to shoot on a city street.

"Students practice responsible use of technology systems, information, and software."

Example: When preparing the school's video yearbook, the media production class verifies their information before taping, carefully sets up and dismantles their equipment, and reviews the features of the software before using it.

"Students develop positive attitudes toward technology uses that support lifelong learning, collaboration, personal pursuits, and productivity."

Example: After videotaping and editing the school musical, a student from the media class offers to videotape and produce a video of her cousin's wedding using her family's equipment.

"Standard III—Technology Productivity Tools"

"Students use technology tools to enhance learning, increase productivity, and promote creativity."

Example: A student in the 10th-grade speech class gave his speech on traffic safety and included a short video on student driving as they leave and enter the school parking lot.

"Students use productivity tools to collaborate in constructing technology-enhanced models, prepare publications, and produce other creative works."

Example: Four students in the high school business class work together to produce an advertisement of their school store and play it over the school closed-circuit TV system.

"Standard IV—Technology Communications Tools"

"Students use a variety of media and formats to communicate information and ideas effectively to multiple audiences."

Example: Students in the American history class create a local history video that incorporates still photos, regional music, and personal narrative of longtime residence of the area along with the recorded video.

"Reprinted with permission from *National Education Technology Standards for Students: Connecting Curriculum and Technology,* copyright © 2000, ISTE (International Society for Technology in Education), 800.336.5191 (U.S. & Canada) or 541.302.3777 (International), <www.iste.org, iste@iste.org>. All rights reserved. Permission does not constitute an endorsement by ISTE."

Applying Digital Video to the Information Literacy Standards

Foreseeing the tremendous changes that technology and visual and media literacy would have on information literacy, in 1998 The American Association of School Librarians (AASL) and the Association for Educational Communications and Technology (AECT) developed standards to assist library media specialists and other educators in helping students become lifelong learners.

Visual literacy is a large component in information literacy, and the use of digital video is a powerful tool in helping students achieve the Information Literacy Standards.

The following standards and indicators are excerpted from chapter two, "Information Literacy Standards for Student Learning," of *Information Power: Building Partnerships for Learning.*

"Standard Two—The student who is information literate evaluates information critically and competently."

"Indicator 1. Determines accuracy, relevance and comprehensiveness"

By learning to manipulate video-editing software, and evaluating their own videos along with those of their classmates, students will be better able to transfer that same evaluation skill to the professional videos they view on a regular basis. By creating their own video, students will become able to determine the accuracy, relevance, and comprehensiveness of commercially prepared videos.

"Indicator 3. Identifies inaccurate and misleading information"

In preparing a storyboard for a video production, students must select the information to include, what to leave out, and how that information might be slanted. In mastering this process, students will realize how those decisions will affect the accuracy and bias of their presentation. After students have had the opportunity to persuade others using digital video, they will become more conscious of how others may try to manipulate or influence them using digital video.

"Standard Three—The student who is information literate uses information accurately and creatively."

"Indicator 1. Organizes information for practical application"

While storyboarding, editing, and rearranging video clips in a logical format to present information in the most creative and influential manner, students achieve mastery of Indicator 1.

"Indicator 2. Integrates new information into one's own knowledge"

Students bring their own background knowledge, whether it is in a content area or technology, to every learning experience. As students research information and learn new skills in the development of digital video, that new information will automatically be incorporated into their previous knowledge base.

"Indicator 3. Applies information in critical thinking and problem solving"

Developing a digital video is a complex project; critical thinking and problem solving in both the content area and technology must be applied in order for a video to be successful.

"Indicator 4. Produces and communicates information and ideas in appropriate formats"

While developing a digital video, students learn the strengths and weaknesses of the video format and when video would be the best format to meet the needs of their audience, or if another format might be better.

"Standard Five—The student who is an independent learner is information literate and appreciates literature and other expressions of information."

"Indicator 2. Derives meaning from information presented creatively in a variety of formats"

Students who work with digital video become proficient in Indicator 2 as they make use of the wide variety of editing features available in the editing software and realize how the use of those features helps others derive information from their video.

"Indicator 3. Develops creative products in a variety of formats"

By identifying and using video that matches the ideas and emotions that they wish to communicate, students become proficient in Indicator 3.

"Standard Seven—The student who contributes positively to the learning community and to society is information literate and recognizes the importance of information to a democratic society."

"Indicator 1. Seeks information from diverse sources, contexts, disciplines, and cultures"

Students who create digital video become proficient in mastering Indicator 1 as they seek information from diverse sources and contexts to incorporate into their projects.

"Standard Eight—The student who contributes positively to the learning community and to society is information literate and practices ethical behavior in regard to information and information technology."

"Indicator 2. Respects intellectual property rights"

Students learn to respect the intellectual property rights of others when they obtain copyright permission needed and give credit where credit is due. As library media specialists and teachers assist students in obtaining and combining various audio and video clips, the students will become proficient in Indicator 2.

"Indicator 3. Use information technology responsibly"

When students are given the opportunity to operate digital video equipment, they learn responsibility in the care and maintenance of that equipment and become proficient in Indicator 3.

"Standard Nine—The student who contributes positively to the learning community and to society is information literate and participates effectively in groups to pursue and generate information."

"Indicator 1. Shares knowledge and information with others"

Students using digital video share knowledge and information, both with their audience and with other students working on the same video project.

"Indicator 2. Respects others' ideas and backgrounds and acknowledges their contributions"

As students work in groups developing a digital video, they learn to respect the ideas and backgrounds of others and acknowledge the contribution of each team member to the group video.

"Indicator 3. Collaborates with others, both in person and through technologies, to identify information problems and to seek their solutions"

Students become proficient in collaboration in identifying information problems and seeking solutions as they cooperate in a student-produced video.

"Indicator 4. Collaborate with others, both in person and through technologies, to design, develop, and evaluate information products and solutions"

In designing, developing, and producing a digital video with classmates, students achieve mastery of Indicator 4. As students synthesize ideas and evaluate their total digital video-editing experience, they gain confidence in their achievement in both the intellectual and the creative components of their visual communications.

Ethical and Legal Issues of Student-Produced Videos

Nothing is more important to our society than protecting our children. With the ease of mass production of video along with Internet communications, a wealth of local, state, and federal legislation designed to protect our children has been introduced. However, passing legislation that provides a balance between privacy and First Amendment rights has become an extremely controversial issue. Because the enforcement of this legislation can be extremely problematic, it is critical that students receive guidance in making ethical and legal choices independent of the presence of an adult.

District Acceptable Use Policies

Most school districts have an *Acceptable Use Policy* (AUP) to regulate the use of district computers and other technology. Most schools require students and parents to sign written agreements to abide by these policies before the student is allowed to use a school computer to access the Internet.

One of the more sensitive issues covered in AUPs is how to highlight student achievement while protecting a child's privacy. Many AUPs require a parental signature before a student's work is published on the Web, especially those under 13.

Many school districts require written permission from the parents before videotaping any minor, but federal law requires that students in special education programs are not to be videotaped anywhere that identifies them as requiring special help without parental permission.

A well thought out AUP will help avoid problems such as these that happened in one school. To highlight an after-school program obtained through a grant, organizers in the program each videotaped the portion in which they were involved. They gave the collection of video clips to a media specialist to assemble and edit before submitting the video to the grant sponsors. After the video was completed and only a few hours remained before the video was due, one parent objected to having her son in the video even though he was shown mainly from the back. To rectify the difficult situation, the media specialist made a digital blue ball with text that floated around one section of the video that concealed the student in question. The next year the school administration rewrote their AUP.

Children's Online Protection Act (COPA) and Children's Online Privacy Protection Act (COPPA)

Children's Online Protection Act (COPA) and Children's Online Privacy Protection Act (COPPA) must be distinguished from each other. They may work hand in hand, but each legislative act can be modified separately. The importance of these laws should not be underestimated because of their applicability to our most precious resource—children.

The Children's Online Protection Act, (COPA) of 1998 amended the Communications Act of 1934 and was primarily enacted at 47 U.S.C. § 231. COPA's main purpose was to restrict access to any communication, picture, image, graphic image file, article, recording, writing, or other matter of any kind that was blatantly obscene to minors under the age of 18. Violators who knowingly made such materials available to minors for commercial gain over the World Wide Web could be fined more than $50,000, imprisoned not more than six months, or both.

On June 29, 2004, the Supreme Court ruled by a 5-4 vote that the Child Online Protection Act passed in 1998 violates the First Amendment because it would restrict the free-speech rights of adults to see and buy pornography over the Internet. The justices did not toss out the law entirely, but sent the matter back to a lower court to investigate whether improvements in Internet filtering capacity since the law was enacted may provide a less restrictive method.

While COPA sought to protect children from access to certain materials, COPPA was designed to control the collection of personal information from children under the age of 13. COPPA, or the *Children's Online Privacy Protection Act* of 1998, was enacted as 15 U.S.C. § 6501 through § 6506. COPPA prohibits an operator of a Web site or online service from collecting personal information from a child. The Federal Trade Commission (FTC) administers COPPA regulations. Some of the issues included in the Children's Online Privacy Protection Act and Rule apply to individually identifiable information about a child that is collected online, such as full name, home address, e-mail address, telephone number, or any other information that would allow someone to identify or contact the child. The Act and Rule also cover other types of information—for example, hobbies, interests, and information collected through cookies or other types of tracking mechanisms — when they are tied to individually-identifiable information.

When developing a video to be distributed via the World Wide Web, the COPPA Laws will need to be consulted. For detailed information on The Children's Online Privacy Protection Act refer to the Federal Trade Commission Web site <www.ftc.gov/ogc/coppa1.htm>.

The American Library Association has taken a firm stand against filtering and the COPA laws as they relate to the public libraries. How COPA and COPPA should be implemented in school libraries (and schools in general) is a different situation than public libraries. Unlike public libraries, schools (and school libraries) do assume some *in loco parentis* responsibilities. The extent to which a school library media specialist assumes parental responsibilities for students will depend in large part on decisions made by the local school board or superintendent. The role of library media specialists and teachers will also depend on the nature of the resources being used in the classroom and whether those resources require students to divulge personally identifiable information.

Some schools may choose to act *in loco parentis;* other schools may decide to request consent through an Acceptable Use Policy signed by students and parents at the beginning of the year, and others do not take responsibility for online protection, but leave it up to parents. While the application of the COPA and COPPA laws could be approached as purely a philosophical discussion, decisions made by individual schools could either enhance or interfere with curricular instruction.

The Children's Internet Protection Act (CIPA)

The Children's Internet Protection Act (CIPA) was signed into law on December 21, 2000. Under CIPA, no school or library may receive federal funds unless it certifies that it is enforcing a policy of Internet safety that includes the use of filtering or blocking technology. The Internet Safety Policy must protect against Internet access to visual depictions that are obscene, child pornography, or (in the case of use by minors) harmful to minors. The school or library must also certify that it is enforcing the operation of such filtering or blocking technology during any use of such computers by minors.

Details for administering the Children's Internet Protection Act can be found on the Universal Service Administrative Company Homepage <www.sl.universalservice.org/reference/CIPA.asp>. Some schools have decided to forgo federal funding than limit their accessibility to the World Wide Web.

Fair Use Laws

Section 107 of Title 17 of the U.S. Code allows the use of copyrighted work for purposes such as criticism, comment, news reporting, teaching (including multiple copies for classroom use), scholarship, or research. In determining if a particular copyrighted work can be used under the Fair Use Laws, the following factors are taken into consideration.

1. "the purpose and character of the use, including whether such use is of a commercial nature or is for nonprofit educational purposes;

2. the nature of the copyrighted work;

3. the amount and substantiality of the portion used in relation to the copyrighted work as a whole; and

4. the effect of the use upon the potential market for or value of the copyrighted work."

For a complete *Reproduction of Copyrighted Works by Educators and Librarians* see <www.copyright.gov/circs/circ21.pdf>.

Copyright guidelines can be confusing at times, but a thumbnail guideline for students or educators is: no more than 10 percent or three minutes (whichever is less) of copyrighted "motion media" is allowed to be integrated into a multimedia or video project. An educator or student may reproduce, perform, and display up to 10 percent of a copyright musical composition in a multimedia program. For more complete summary of copyright laws, refer to <http://www.aea11.k12.ia.us/downloads/copyrightbooklet.pdf >.

Digital Millennium Copyright Act

The Digital Millennium Copyright Act (DMCA) signed into law by President Bill Clinton on October 28, 1998 created two new prohibitions in Title 17 of the U.S. Code. The DMCA covers the circumvention of technological measures used by copyright owners to protect their works, tampering with copyright management information, and adds civil remedies and criminal penalties for violating the prohibitions.

The impact of the DMCA on educators is that it provides exemptions from anti-circumvention provisions for nonprofit libraries, archives, and educational institutions under certain circumstances and limits liability of nonprofit institutions of higher education—when they serve as online service providers and under certain circumstances—for copyright infringement by faculty members or graduate students.

For details of the Digital Millennium Copyright Act, consult <www.loc.gov/copyright/legislation/dmca.pdf>.

Obtaining Copyright Clearance

Several Internet sites are available to help users obtain copyright permission on specific works, if a work is covered under the Fair Use Laws. The most commonly used site is the Copyright Clearance Center at <www.copyright.com/>. Here a person can obtain permission to reproduce copyrighted content such as articles and book chapters, Web sites, e-mail, and more.

Copyright for photographs can be obtained through the Media Image Resource Alliance (MIRA) <http://mira.com/>. MIRA is a Stock Agency of Creative Eye, a cooperative of independent artists and photographers, where a consumer can purchase the right to use an image according to the cooperative's copyright license.

The Harry Fox Agency, Inc. <www.harryfox.com/> provides a musical copyright information source and licensing agency. Schools, churches, community groups and other low-volume producers of music CDs or cassettes can easily and quickly obtain a license online at "Songfile" <www.songfile.com/>, sponsored by the Harry Fox Agency.

A video clip copyright license can be obtained at Motion Picture Licensing Corporation (MPLC) <http://www.mplc.com/index2.htm>. The MPLC is an independent copyright licensing service exclusively authorized by major Hollywood motion picture studios and independent producers to grant blanket licenses to non-profit groups, businesses, and government organizations for the public performances of home videocassettes and DVDs.

For additional resources for obtaining copyright permission, contact the Youth Video Distribution Toolkit at <www.ymdi.org/toolkit/archives/000491.php>. The YMDi's mission is to improve the distribution of independent youth created film, video, radio, and new media and provides a wealth of information and tools that are essential to increasing the visibility of youth-made media.

Teaching the complexities of copyright ethics to students can be extremely challenging. It can best be taught by modeling respect for the intellectual property of the author or producer of a work. Many online sites have been developed to assist educators in teaching copyright ethics. One of the most popular is *Welcome to Copyright Kids!* <http://www.copyrightkids.org/>.

To avoid the complexities of obtaining copyright clearance, many royalty-free commercial companies are available. When purchasing royalty-free music, the buyer receives music that can be used and distributed in any way desired with limited restrictions.

Music and lyrics written by an American author and published in 1922 or earlier are in the public domain in the United States. No one can claim ownership of a song in the public domain; therefore, public-domain songs may be used by everyone. Public-domain songs are available for profit making without paying any royalties. If a new version or derivative of a public-domain song is made, that version of the song can be copyrighted, and no one can use it without permission. However, the original song remains in the public domain, and anyone else can make and copyright his own version of the same public-domain song. A reference site to help identify public domain songs and public domain music is found at <http://www.pdinfo.com/>.

Students need to become aware that just because a photo is on the Internet does not necessarily mean it is copyright cleared. To provide copyright-cleared photos some schools subscribe to royalty-free clipart, animation, font, and sound libraries at <http://schools.clipart.com/> or individuals can subscribe to <http://clipart.com>.

The Library of Congress provides American Memory: the National Digital Library at <http://memory.loc.gov/>, which contains a wealth of historical sound, video, and still images in digital format. Images are continually being updated on this site and students should be encouraged to check this site regularly for additional digital files.

Pics4Learning is a copyright-friendly image library for teachers and students <http://www.pics4learning.com/>. The Pics4Learning collection consists of thousands of images that have been donated by students, teachers, and amateur photographers. Tech4Learning and the Orange County Public Schools Technology Development Unit developed Pics4Learning as part of the Partners in Education program.

Visual literacy in education covers a wide range of issues, has a tremendous impact on student learning, and has a great impact on communication skills. Several organizations such as the Center for Media Literacy and the International Visual Literacy Association provide clear and concise interpretation and articulation of the theory and issues in media and visual literacy. The International Society of Technology in Education (ISTE) has provided standards for teachers, students, and administrators to help meet those challenges.

This increased use of technology multiplies the ethical and legal issues library media specialists and teachers must face each day as they encourage the use of student-produced videos. Fair Use Laws had been taught in most teacher preparation programs along with an introduction to obtaining copyright clearance. Now, educators are faced with an alphabet soup of legislation governing children and the use of technology. It has become vital that all educators be familiar with the Children's Online Protection Act (COPA) and Children's Online Privacy Protection Act (COPPA), The Children's Internet Protection Act (CIPA), and the Digital Millennium Copyright Act (DMCA).

Visual, media, and information literacy provide the cornerstone for the use of technology in education. With visual, media, and information literacy, students will be able to strengthen their skills in various content areas and learn skills that will last them a lifetime.

Chapter 2

Selecting Hardware

History of Video and the Conversion from Analog to Digital

In order to understand 21st century technology, it is necessary to understand from where and how fast technology evolved in the 20th century. The challenge for educators is that information is multiplying so fast that even specialists in the particular field have trouble keeping up.

In 1923 Vladimir Kosma Zworykin invented the first video capture device called the *iconoscope,* which measured a meager one square inch. Four years later, Philo Taylor Farnsworth transmitted an image of 60 horizontal lines. Using Farnsworth's equipment, the 1936 Berlin Olympics became the first televised sporting event in world history.

The 1930s television consisted of an electron beam scanning horizontal lines across a cathode ray tube creating a picture. Television in the 1930s and 1940s, when it was not broadcast live, used film cameras pointed at video monitors to record footage. This process was called *kinescoping*.

Analog technology attempts to duplicate the source with voltage waveforms. The AMPEX Corporation invented the first competent video recording device based on magnetic recording principles in the 1950s. The 1956 National Association of Broadcasters (NAB) is considered the birth of video recording.

In 1975 Sony launched the first consumer video recorder, called the *Betamax*. A year later JVC released a competing video recording format called *VHS*. While Sony's Beta had better video quality, it was eventually overtaken by VHS. The failure of Sony's Beta was due to market politics and hardware limitations.

An analog recording device writes the waveforms magnetically to tape. The quality of the recording depends on a multitude of factors, but the ultimate weakness of analog technology is format instability. Every time a person records a copy from the original tape, the waveform does not reproduce exactly, resulting in deterioration from the original.

Analog home video became a reality in the early 1980s and consumers were able to record home movies with sound that could be played back on any VCR. As the home camcorder market grew, several analog formats emerged. 8mm, VHS-C, and later Hi-8 offered home users better video quality in increasingly smaller camcorder sizes.

Since 1997, electronics stores have contained an ever-increasing number of digital video camcorders while their financial investment continues to spiral downward. At the same time, home computers have become fast enough to perform powerful video editing. This combination has increased creative options exponentially.

The foundation of computers and digital technology is the *bit*. A bit is represented by two states—*off* and *on* (in computer code, *zero* and *one).* Just as zeroes and ones can be used to represent letters, they can also be used to represent images, sounds, and moving video. The advantage of digital data is that the sequence of zeroes and ones can be exactly reproduced, unlike analog data that loses quality with each reproduction.

Since we are slowly approaching a new television format called *HDTV*, future compatibility may become a concern. Consumers need to be cautious of investing in a new digital video format that lacks market acceptance along with formats that lack a *Firewire* port. Before a major financial investment in video equipment is made, the consumer should first evaluate the need, the features of the device, and the projected future of the desired format. Many closets and garage sales are full of electronic devices that were purchased before a serious evaluation of the need and future of an item was made.

Selecting Camcorders

One of the first considerations when beginning a digital video project is the selection of a camcorder. Video shot with a camcorder fits into one of two categories, analog or digital. Analog video is delivered using a constantly changing electrical signal while digital signals are encoded in a binary format where each bit of information is represented as a one or a zero. The primary advantage of a digital video signal is that it does not degrade during duplication and can be easily manipulated and edited.

Analog camcorders come in four formats. VHS is the most familiar. It offers the low quality of about 250 lines of resolution on a 1/2-inch tape. The length of these tapes comes in 30-minute, 60-minute, and 120-minute each in EP (extended play), SLP (slow play), and SP (standard play) formats.

The *S-VHS* (super VHS) format was developed for videographers who desired a higher-quality picture. S-VHS contains more than 400 lines of resolution, but the down side is that S-VHS cannot be played on the popular VHS VCR. Super-video (aka S-video or S-VHS) uses a special connector called an S-video (or YC or S-VHS) jack. This special connection breaks the video signal into *chrominance* (color) and *luminance* (brightness). S-video allows for better transfer of video, but does not transfer audio.

The *VHS-C* (VHS-compact) format couples the VHS format with a smaller-size camcorder. The VHS-C camcorder is held in one hand and uses a VHS-C videotape, which is about half the size of regular VHS tape. The tapes can be played in regular VHS VCRs using a special videocassette adapter.

Hi-8 and *8mm* use small videotape eight millimeters wide. Picture quality rivals S-VHS for resolution and clarity. Hi-8 contains 400 lines resolution while 8mm format cameras contain no more than 240 lines. Both formats were designed to be operated from the palm of the hand. The downside is that Hi-8 and 8mm VCRs are required for playback and editing and may not be as available as the VHS VCRs, so most projects will have to be transferred to VHS for home viewing.

The VHS, VHS-C, Hi-8, and 8mm cameras use composite video jacks that connect to VCRs or TVs. Composite cables handle all the signal information as one big wavelength. The yellow cable carries the video signal, and the red-and-white cables carry the two audio channels (right and left).

Digital video (DV) is dramatically better than the older analog standards. DV is identical to the original footage. DV in = DV out. *Digital8* is a proprietary (Sony only) format that is used to record digital video onto Hi-8 style tapes. Digital8 camcorders by Sony range between $500 and $1,000. They have lower video quality (still better than analog) and fewer bells and whistles. However, they still possess the advantages of DV—a lossless video compression and the ability to input video easily into a computer. One advantage of Digital8 is tape costs: five-dollar 8mm tapes are half the price of MiniDV tapes.

MiniDV is a growing standard of the Digital Video format, and most digital video cameras record in this format. The MiniDV camcorders priced in the budget range ($500-$1,000) have quality limitations similar to those that affect Digital8 camcorders but are much smaller since the MiniDV tape is smaller. Due to their small size, DV camcorders can be hard to keep steady. The smaller size of DV cameras also affects sound quality because everything is so close together, and they are more prone to picking up motor noise on the recordings.

Sony has recently developed an even smaller format in the MICROMV with 70 percent smaller tape cartridges, and cameras that weigh less than one pound. The MICROMV cassette is smaller than a matchbox, or about the size of two quarters, or smaller and thinner than half a MiniDV cassette.

As this kind of equipment gets smaller and smaller, however, there comes a point when the trade-offs become too severe. The LCD screens get too small to view details and the buttons become too tiny to control reliably with normal-sized fingers.

Because of the reduced size, there is less tape surface in the cartridge, which means fewer bits available to store an hour of video on a tape. As a result, MICROMV requires a more aggressive compression of the video data. Concerning quality and usability, the MICROMV camcorders have received mixed reviews.

Regardless of the purchasing budget, there are many factors to keep in mind when buying a new video camera. Digital camcorders use a chip called a *charge coupled device* (CCD) to capture the image behind the lens. A CCD has thousands or millions of pixels that translate the image it receives into a digital picture—the more pixels, the higher the resolution, the sharper the picture.

The main difference between single-chip and three-chip (CCD) camcorders is the quality of the image produced. Manufacturers of single-chip camcorders may compensate for the lack of color clarity by including an *RGB* (Red-Green-Blue) primary color filter. This filter separates light passing through the lens into the three primary color components assisting in the color reproduction. However, even with a RGB primary color filter, the video produced by single-chip camcorders cannot match the quality of those produced by three CCD camcorders.

While more CCDs are always the best, the main consideration is how much color clarity is actually needed. Will the camera usage warrant the added financial investment? If possible, a school will want a camera with three CCDs, instead of one.

In considering a hybrid video/still camera, the user must be ready to sacrifice quality on the still-camera side. Therefore, buying a separate still camera and video camcorder is recommended. Even the best camcorders perform modestly when compared to low-end still cameras.

Today's camcorders generally offer a flip-out, side-mounted LCD that allows the user to hold the camera away from the body so they can observe the surroundings, preventing unexpected activity within the frame of the video. The downside of using an LCD viewfinder is that it uses a great deal of battery power.

When selecting a digital camcorder the following specifications should be considered: format: Digital8 or MiniDV; number of CCDs (charge coupled device); resolution (the closer to 550 lines, the better the video quality); image stabilizer; type and number of input/output connectors; input for external microphone; ability to capture still images; external LCD monitor size; colored viewfinder; optical zoom (optical zoom is handled within the lens itself while digital zoom is handled inside the brains of the camcorder); type of battery; and price.

Selecting Video Capture Cards

During the next several years, there will be a blending of formats while the consumer converts from analog to digital formats. In order to convert analog signal from a VHS camera or a VCR to a digital signal, a computer will need a video capture card with a composite port. To capture from a Hi-8 or S-VHS camera, the video card will need an S-video port.

Video capture cards come pre-installed on the newer Macs, but separate capture cards may need to be installed on PCs. To check if there is a video capture card, one needs to turn the computer around and look at the ports. If there is a round port labeled 'Video In' (probably with a yellow ring around it), then the computer has a video capture card. If not, a video capture card will need to be installed before the user can convert analog to digital and digital to analog.

The older the computer, the more difficult it can be to add a video capture card, but that does not mean one will have to purchase a new computer in order to capture analog video. It just means that more research is needed to find a compatible capture card.

Most video capture cards connect to either an internal PCI or AGP slot inside the computer or externally via the USB port. Some Web cams can also be used for video capture, but they tend to be of such low quality as not to be worth considering for serious use.

Analog capture cards use various compression methods, called codecs (COmpression/DECompression), to digitize and pack the video onto the hard drive. The more expensive capture cards have chips on the card that compress the video. Some form of video compression is essential, since it takes over two gigabytes of hard drive space to store nine one-half minutes of uncompressed video. Compression on a capture card removes the need for the PC to do the actual compressing of the video. The capture cards with compression chips can usually offer higher resolution capture and will work almost irrespective of the power of the underlying PC (within reason).

Capture cards have their own software that must have a workable relationship with the video-editing software. Most companies that make video capture cards create their own proprietary file format. It is important to know the specifications of the particular capture card's format, such as frame size, frame rate, and data rate. For example, if the video capture card can capture video at 352 pixels wide by 240 pixels high, then it would not be a good choice to try to convert the video back to 720 by 480 pixels (this is what the DV format uses). In this situation, the video quality would be poor because the user starts out with a smaller video frame.

Instead of opening the computer case and installing an internal capture card, some choose USB capture devices that consist of a USB lead with a small plastic box containing the electronics and connectors. Such USB devices usually contain TV and composite jacks or S-video only. This type of conversion box is used with a laptop or if all the PCI slots inside the PC are already used. The quality from video capture on a USB card is not as high as an internal card since the USB interface is not designed to transfer the large amounts of data and the video has to be highly compressed before it is sent through the USB cable.

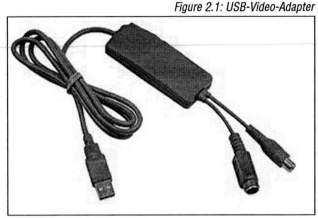

Figure 2.1: USB-Video-Adapter

If an internal capture card with built-in hardware compression is not an option, one can still capture high-quality, high-resolution analog video by using a DV Bridge, such as *Dazzle*, to convert incoming analog signal into digital video using a standard Firewire card. Dazzle tends to be more expensive than an analog capture card with hardware compression, but it can be money well spent.

A Dazzle is an external box that connects to the computer via a Firewire cable. It contains digital input/output jacks that allow the DV Bridge to serve as a pass through device for a digital camera. The Dazzle also contains RCA jacks for analog input. When the RCA jacks are used, the Dazzle box serves as an analog to digital converter. Some models of Dazzle not only capture analog signal and convert it to digital before sending it to the computer, but they can also convert the digital signal from the computer to analog so the video can be transferred back to a VCR via RCA cables.

Figure 2.2: Dazzle

For optimum video capture, a digital camcorder is needed. A digital camcorder provides the ability to transfer video between the camcorder and computer digitally via Firewire without any compression loss. DV In = DV Out. Today with a DV or Digital8 camcorder and a Firewire card, a person can produce broadcast-quality video that looks as good as the original footage. Firewire ports are extremely fast, capable of transferring up to 400 million bits of data per second.

If a person wants to convert Super-8 videos to digital videos, they will first have to record the video from an analog screen using a DV camcorder. Every DV camcorder has a DV output that can transfer the recorded video footage to a PC. Unlike analog connectors, the DV camcorder port is bi-directional, i.e., it is both an input and an output port.

Selecting Cables and Connectors

Audio and video equipment can be arranged to work together in complex configurations. Most equipment used in audio and video production has various inputs and outputs used to make a variety of connections. A receptacle for a wire is called a *jack* and the connector that is inserted into the jack is called a *plug*. An *adapter* is a small connector that allows conversion from one type of jack or plug to another type. Most electronic stores stock a wide variety of adapters that can convert one type of plug or jack to another.

Cables may have different connectors on each end, effectively translating from, say, three RCA plugs (video, left, and right audio) into a single RCA-mini. When a cable has the same connectors at both ends, it acts as an extension cord. But with different connectors at each end, it becomes a translation cord.

Shielded cables are insulated cables used in audio and video production while unshielded cables have little or no insulation and are used primarily as a stereo speaker or headphone cable. The extra cable insulation maintains signal strength and blocks interference from outside sources such as televisions, computers, and fluorescent lights.

Guidelines for Selecting Cables:

- Match the cables. Two cables may look similar but have very different electrical properties. Minor variations in resistances or shielding capacity may make a significant difference.

- Do not use cheap cables.

- Keep the cables as short as possible. Overly long cables can eventually cause ground hum. If a cable is extremely bunched up, the quality of the audio will be affected.

- Select good shielding. Cables should have stable insulation including a tightly braided shield that is kept snug by the outer jacket so that it is less likely to become loose and short out.

- Keep audio cables away from power cables. If the cables that carry the music are laid across the cables that carry electricity, static or distortions may affect the audio.

Common Types of Audio/Video Connections

Figure 2.3: Composite Jack and Plug

The *RCA composite analog connector* handles all the signal information as one big wavelength. The yellow cable carries the video signal, and the red and white cables carry the two audio channels (right and left). A variation on the RCA plug is the *RCA mini jack* (also called the *headphone jack* or *1/4-inch jack),* which is popular for analog audio output on many consumer devices.

The *S-video* carries separate chroma and luminance signals but no audio.

Figure 2.4: S-Video Jack and Plug

The *IEEE 1394* or *Firewire* connects the camera to the computer using a 4pin connector into the camera side, and 6pin into the Firewire PCI-slot card.

The *RF* (or *F connector* or *BNC connector*) is used with *coaxial ("coax") cables* that are standard for professionals and are common in homes and offices wired for cable television and for connecting a VCR to a television. It is unique in its twist-lock connection.

The *XLR audio connector* connects directly from a microphone to the camera with a three-prong connector (male) on one end, and a connector with three holes in it (female) on the other end. Usually there is a little button to push down so the cable can be inserted, and a snap is heard when the microphone is in place.

The *1/8-inch mini-stereo connector* was created to accommodate the personal, pocket-sized electronics market. A 1/8-inch mini-jack will often plug right into the camera, but these microphones are usually of lower quality than a microphone with an XLR connector.

If necessary, an XLR to mini-jack adapter cable can be used to connect a more expensive microphone into the 1/8-inch mini-jack plug in the camera. However, the adapter cable is thick and tends to put a lot of stress on the plug in the camera.

A *1/4-inch phone connector* is usually used to connect music sources. It can be distinguished by the three parts on the shaft of the plug referred to as the tip, ring, and sleeve. Phone plugs are often found in pairs; one for the right audio channel and another for the left.

The *component connectors* and video cables are similar to RCA cables except they are used with progressive, interlaced, or high-definition video signals. Component analog is the un-encoded output of a camera, videotape recorder consisting of three primary color signals: green, blue, and red (GBR) that together convey all necessary picture information. In some component video formats, these three components have been translated into a luminance signal and two color-difference signals. Component digital is a digital representation of a component analog signal set.

The *digital audio* or *SP/DIF* (The Sony Phillips Digital Interface) *connector* is the most common type of digital interface. The SP/DIF inputs for many sound cards contain coaxial RCA connections using copper wire to transmit audio data. Most high-end SP/DIF connections use an optical signal to transmit the audio signal.

The *lanc* (or *digital I/O*) *connector* allows control data (but not video) to move between the camera and an external device.

The *speaker connectors* and wires carry the amplified signal from the receiver's (or amp's) output terminals to the speaker's input terminals. Speaker wire consists of two leads, typically encased and bundled in plastic insulation, one for the positive signal and one for the negative. The speaker wire will probably be marked (+) and (-) to help distinguish the two leads. If they are not present, there will be no way visually to tell them apart. Its *American Wire Gauge* (AWG, or usually just "gauge" number) identifies the thickness of a wire's conductive copper bundle; the lower

Figure 2.5: Firewire Jack and Plug

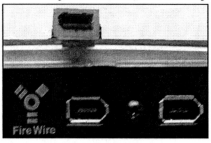

Figure 2.6: RF Jack and Plug

Figure 2.7: XLR Jack and Plug

Figure 2.8: Mini-Jack Plug

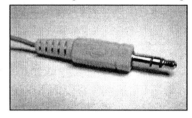

Figure 2.9: One-Fourth Plug

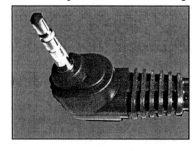

Figure 2.10: Component Cable

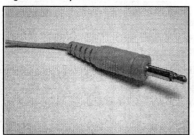

Figure 2.11: Speaker

the gauge, the thicker the wire, and the better its capacity to pass the amplified audio signal. Most speaker wires available on the market today range in thickness from 12 gauge to 16 gauge.

Selecting Microphones

Audio is often overlooked and underemphasized at the school level. Learning how to select and use external microphones will greatly improve a school video since the camcorder microphone is not ideal for every shooting situation. The microphone one uses depends on the circumstances of production. The main drawback to using the interior camcorder microphone is the motor drive noise it picks up due to the camera's compact size.

Many newer camcorders feature a hot accessory shoe, which enables the operator to use proprietary microphones. Proprietary microphones transfer the audio signal through the hot shoe so the user does not need to attach an extra cable.

The primary consideration in selecting a microphone is the element, the part of a microphone that gathers the sound and converts it into electrical audio signal that can be processed by camcorders and audio mixers. Two types of elements used by microphones found in most schools are *"dynamic"* and *"condenser"*.

Dynamic microphones do not require electricity to operate. Because the dynamic microphone requires so little power, the energy source actually comes from the mixer or camera to which it is connected. This is called phantom power. Dynamic microphones are renowned for their ruggedness and reliability. They are less sensitive and usually lack the frequency response of condenser microphones; therefore, dynamic microphones work best with moderate to loud sounds and do not pick up unwanted peripheral noise. Stage microphones tend to be dynamic because they are less sensitive to handling.

A dynamic microphone operates like a speaker "in reverse". Sound pressure moves the diaphragm. This moves the coil, which causes current to flow as lines of flux from the magnet are cut. Instead of putting electrical energy into the coil (as in a speaker), energy comes out. Many intercom systems use small speakers with lightweight cones as both speaker and microphone, by simply switching the same transducer from one end of the amplifier to the other.

On the other hand, condenser microphones require power and are more sensitive to sound. They are preferred for their uniform and wider frequency response and ability to respond with clarity to transient sounds such as music, voice, and special news reports. Except for situations where the operator can get the microphone within inches of the sound source, the operator will want to use some kind of a condenser microphone.

Condenser (or capacitor) microphones use a lightweight membrane and a fixed plate that act as opposite sides of a capacitor. Sound pressure against this thin polymer film causes it to move. This movement changes the capacitance of the circuit, creating a changing electrical output. <http://www.audiotechnica.com/using/mphones/guide/micodes.html>

Condenser elements are the ideal (or the only) choice for many applications because they weigh much less than dynamic elements and they can be much smaller. These characteristics make them the logical choice for line or "shotgun" microphones, lavalieres, and miniature microphones of all types.

In addition to classifying microphones by their generating elements, they are also identified by how well they pick up sound from various directions. Most microphones can be placed into one of two main groups: *omni-directional* (or cardioid) and *directional* (or unidirectional).

Omni-directional microphones are the simplest to design, build, and understand. They pick up sound from just about every direction equally. The physical size of the omni-directional microphone has a direct bearing on how well the microphone maintains its omni-directional characteristics at very high frequencies. The body of the microphone simply blocks the shorter high-frequency wavelengths that arrive from the rear. The smaller the microphone body diameter, the closer the microphone can come to being truly omni-directional.

Directional microphones are specially designed to respond best to sound from the front (and rear in the case of bi-directional), while tending to reject sound that arrives from other directions. This effect also varies with frequency, and only the better microphones are able to provide uniform rejection over a wide range of frequencies. This directional ability is usually the result of external openings and internal passages in the microphone that allow sound to reach both sides of the diaphragm in a carefully controlled way. Sound arriving from the front of the microphone will aid diaphragm motion, while sound arriving from the side or rear will cancel diaphragm motion.

Figure 2.12: Microphone Pick-up Patterns

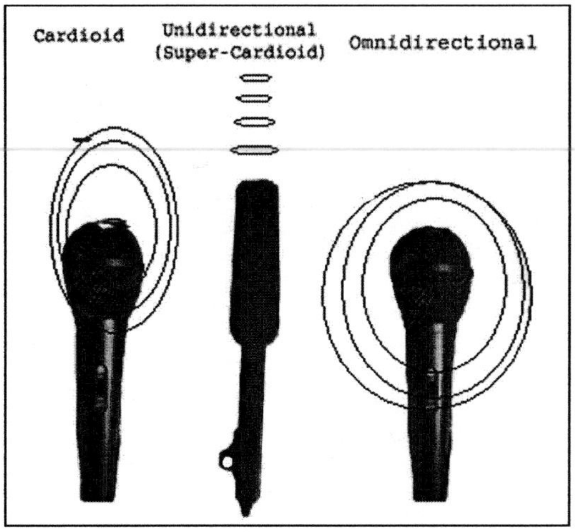

When is it best to use which sound pattern? Whether an operator selects a directional or omni-directional microphone depends on the application (recording versus sound reinforcement), the acoustic conditions, the working distance required, and the kind of sound desired.

Directional microphones can suppress unwanted noise, reduce the effects of reverberation, and increase gain-before-feedback. However, in good acoustic surroundings, omni-directional microphones, properly placed, can preserve the "sound" of the recording location, and are often preferred for their flatness of response and freedom from proximity effect.

Omni-directional microphones are normally better at resisting wind noise and mechanical or handling noise than directional microphones. Omnis are also less susceptible to "popping" caused by certain explosive consonants in speech, such as "p", "b", and "t".

Most Common Types of Microphones

The *on-camera microphone* is built onto the camcorder. This small microphone is about 1.5 inches long and is omni-directional. The microphone built into the camera is good for ambient audio or natural sound such as nature scenes like chirping birds or babbling brooks, or background noise from street scene. On-camera microphones can be used to record a performance or a speech, although the quality of the audio will suffer because of all the other ambient sounds it picks up.

The *lavaliere microphone* is a small microphone, about an inch tall, that can be clipped onto a piece of clothing about four inches below the speaker's mouth. A thin cord attaches the microphone to a battery pack that the speaker can put in his pocket or clip onto his clothing. Because it is not directly attached to the camera, it is called a "wireless" microphone. A lavaliere microphone is useful when capturing the sound of the speaker and is generally used when the speaker is moving around, versus sitting still or standing at a podium. These microphones will screen out most ambient sound.

When using a lavaliere microphone, operators should always have an extra AA battery on hand so that the microphone will not go dead in the middle of an interview. One sign

Figure 2.13: Lavaliere

Figure 2.14: Handheld

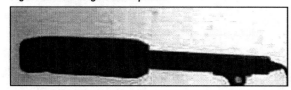

Figure 2.15: Shotgun Microphone

Figure 2.16: Tripod

💡 **Tip**

In general, it is best to do the camera movements such as zoom in, zoom out, pan, or tilt before the scene is shot. It is important that camera operators know how to adjust the height of the camcorder.

that a battery is getting low on a lavaliere microphone is that that operator will start to hear a crackling sound in the headphones.

The *handheld microphone* is a microphone attached to the camera by a long cable or a wireless system. As the name implies, the user holds the microphone while speaking, singing, or interviewing someone. It can also be placed into a table or floor stand while a person is speaking at a podium or in front of the class. Handheld microphones are usually cardioid microphones, which means they have a somewhat heart-shaped sound pick-up pattern. They capture sound directly in front of the microphone better than sound to the sides or back.

The *shotgun microphone* (also known as *line microphone*) is a long, unidirectional microphone designed to pick up sound at a distance. The line microphone uses an interference tube in front of the element to ensure much greater cancellation of sound arriving from the sides. For example, if a person wants to record people 30 feet away, the shotgun microphone must be pointed directly at them. However, the range of a shotgun microphone will vary. This type of microphone is often used at sporting activities or in preparing video and film, in order to pick up sound when the microphone must be located outside the viewing angle of the camera.

Selecting Tripods

A *tripod* is a three-legged camcorder (or camera) stand that enables the operator to raise or lower the camcorder, pivot up and down or right and left (also called *panning*), and tilt. A tripod provides a firm base for the camcorder since the strongest, most experienced videographers can comfortably hold a steady shot for no more than a minute or two. Using tripods, videographers and photographers can improve the sharpness of their shots and increase the variety of conditions in which they shoot, such as night or low light.

There are two types of head units on a tripod, fluid head and friction head. A friction head creates resistance by pushing metal against metal. A fluid head floats on a bed of oil or some other viscous fluid. Friction heads are not as smooth as fluid heads, but they are also cheaper.

The up or down placement lever of the tripod head is called *pedestal*. The pedestal should not be confused with the tilt knob. The tilt knob changes only the up, down angle of the camera while the pedestal knob changes the up or down placement of the entire camera on the tripod head.

Quality tripods have a fluid head. The fluid head has a thick, oily substance that makes smooth pans and tilts easy to do. The operator can position the bubble either inside a circle or between two lines on a tube. By moving the bubble to its correct position, the camera becomes perpendicular to the gravitational pull of the Earth. This results in being able to pan the camera 360 degrees while keeping the horizon straight in the frame. The user can position the bubble by raising or lowering the tripod legs or by adjusting the tripod's head—if the head attaches to the tripod with a claw ball. The latter allows the user to loosen the head and position the leveling bubble without touching the legs.

Considerations in Selecting a Tripod

Figure 2.17: Quick-Release Assembly

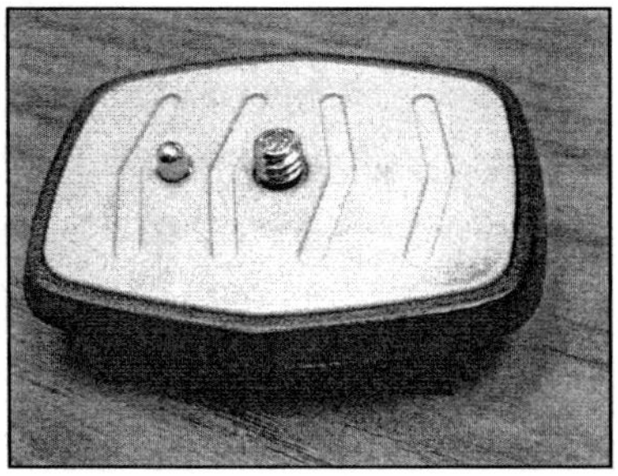

When considering the purchase of a tripod, the following questions should be asked. What is the weight of the camera? Can the tripod be fitted with wheels or casters to allow it to roll smoothly across the floor? For outdoor use, does it have metal spikes in the feet, for a solid interface to the ground? Does it contain a quick-release assembly? (Screwing the camera into a tripod can be a time-consuming, knuckle-bruising experience.) The tripods with these assemblies include a special plate or post that screw into the bottom of the camera. That plate or post can be attached quickly and conveniently to the tripod, and without that assembly, the tripod is useless.

Tripods come with certain built-in problems: They require a lot of floor space and are unwieldy to retract and set up. For shooting situations where a traditional tripod is not usable, there is the monopod. The monopod is a one-legged camcorder (or camera) stabilizer/stand. Monopods can be set up quickly and require no more floor space than a quarter. They are obviously not as stable as a tripod, but some of them have a swing-down foot, making an "L" at ground level, which adds stability.

Selecting Lights

The camcorder light is the most convenient external lighting option since it enables the operator to shoot in mildly low-lit situations. However, built-in camera lights are limited by size. They can display a relatively narrow beam, which is acceptable for shooting close-up scenes with a few people in the frame. However, if the on-camera light is used too close to a person's face, the person tends to squint from the intense added light.

Professional-grade lighting sets are extremely costly and often outside a school budget. Clip-on utility lamps can be purchased in a hardware store and photoflood incandescent light bulbs with different wattages can provide various levels of brightness types and colors of light that are often more realistic. Utility lights can be clipped to stands or held by students during production.

A DIY (Do It Yourself) light kit can be purchased at a local hardware store. It has a 1,000-watt Dual Head telescoping tripod work light (composed of two 500-watt lights) for around $50. Each 500-watt halogen light can be turned on and off separately. The wire cage heat protectors may cast shadows, but they can be removed if desired. However, if working around young students, for safety's sake the heat protectors might be worth the shadows.

To add functionality, an inline dimmer ($5-$40), which allows the user to adjust precisely the intensity of the light, can be added to the power cord to the light. To install an inline dimmer, a user needs to splice the power cord, connect the wires, and insulate the connection with electrical tape.

Reflectors are helpful in bouncing natural light back onto the subject to lessen the shadows created by direct sunlight. Professional-grade reflectors are extremely expensive for school projectors, but collapsible car dashboard sun blockers can provide durable, inexpensive reflectors. Other possibilities for reflectors include making them from three 3" by 3" sheets of one-inch white foam core board, oven-broiler-grade aluminum foil, and masking tape. Collapsible cloth reflectors are even more convenient.

Selecting Lens Filters

Filters attach on top of the video lens and can be applied and removed as needed. Lens filters that are common for still cameras are also available for the digital camcorder. The learning curve in using filters is high and involves significant cost, but if a video operator is willing to take the time, a professional-looking product can be developed. In spite of a possible 3 percent to 5 percent image resolution loss, the use of filters could be well worth the investment.

The most common filters include:

- Wide-angle lens adapters enable a wider field of vision. (This will enable wider picture without having to take one or two steps back.)

- Telephoto lenses, also called converters, increase the power of the zoom.

- UV or haze filters are used against ultraviolet light. (UV rays show up as a bluish cast.)

- Polarizing filters (polarizer) are used for outdoor photography. They help eliminate glare and bring out colors, especially the blue of the sky.

- Neutral density (ND) filters are used to lower the amount of light coming into the camcorder without having to adjust exposure.

Figure 2.18: Barn Doors

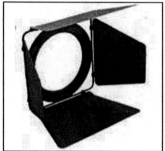

- A lens protector kept permanently on the lens of the camera protects against scratches and chips that would require a costly replacement of the lens itself.

- Scrim is a sheet of spun cotton, wire, or glass that fits in front of the lens to change harsh, directional light into softer, diffused light.

- Barn doors are adjustable black metal flaps that can be attached to some lights to mask off unwanted light and keep it from spilling into areas where it is not needed.

Selecting Computer Systems—PC, MAC, and Turnkey Systems

While there may be serious personal preferences in selecting digital video-editing systems, in reality, the actual differences depend more on the software than the operating system itself. However, there are some real issues to consider in selecting operating systems for non-linear digital editing.

Part of the appeal of the Mac platform is that it is easy to use and has a more stable architecture with fewer compatibility issues with its own software. The common software packages for the Mac include *iMovie* (which is bundled with the iMac DV, iBook, PowerBook, Power Mac G4, and Power Mac G4 Cube). Higher-level software such as *Final Cut Pro* and Adobe *Premiere* can be purchased independently. The drawback of the iMac editing system is that users are not able to expand their system.

On the other hand, a person can spend $100 for an OHCI Firewire capture card, an analog capture card, or an external USB pass-through device to add to an existing PC or purchase a new PC for under $1,000. With these features, a user can end up with about the same editing features as the iMac with much less cost.

With a PC-based system, the user has a wider choice of low-cost software and additional capture devices that can easily be added to the system. For the cost of *Final Cut Pro* for the Mac, a person can get a PC based Real-Time DV card, Adobe *Premiere* video-editing software, and several other additional software packages.

Most educators are limited to what is available at their school and must learn to work within that framework. Almost certainly, whatever an educator has, the odds are strong that within a short time, they will be drooling over the latest and greatest technology.

A digital video-editing turnkey system such as the *Kron Casablanca System* or *Avid System* eliminates hardware and software conflicts. A turnkey system can import video from a multitude of formats, capture video directly from the video camera (digital or otherwise) using a standard composite (RCA), S-video connection, or even a Firewire connection. Once the video is stored on the machine, the user can edit the clips in a number of ways and then record the video project to any video format desired, including DVD. The down side of a turnkey system is that it can cost over $3,500 and can only be used to edit video. A PC or Mac editing system can be used for a multitude of other computer tasks such as word processing, creating a spreadsheet, or accessing the Internet.

Selecting CD and DVD Burners

The *VCD (video compact disc)* format uses a low bit rate MPEG-1 video to achieve approximately 74 minutes of near-VHS video quality. VCDs must be properly written to CD-R format; otherwise, they may be limited to playback only on a CD player. Most CD-burning programs now have a VCD template, which ensures a properly written VCD.

Currently, the most tangible high-quality video-distribution format is the recordable DVD, which is quickly replacing the VHS format played on a VCR. The DVD (digital versatile disc) medium is just an improved CD. Its technology is the same, a laser-scanning disc interpreting a series of ones and zeros. DVD offers a distinct advantage over previous formats with its higher quality and increased storage space. The typical CD-R contains 650 MB while a DVD contains approximately 4.7 GB.

There are two competing DVD formats, DVD-R/RW and DVD+R/RW, each supported by their own manufacturers. Until recent months, most DVD players could only play one format, but that has now changed and now most DVD players are able to automatically detect and play several formats.

"Authoring" is the process of writing video files into a readable media. Most CD and DVD burners come with authoring software, or authoring software such as *Nero*, *GoDVD Plug-In* in Ulead Video Studio, Ulead *MovieFactory*, Sonic *MyDVD*, or Ulead *Movie Studio Pro Director's Cut* can be purchased independently. If a DVD is composed of multiple movie files, the creator will have a main menu with an icon link to each file. If scene links are added, they will exist on secondary menus that will be activated when the main menu link is clicked. Any imported file will play from beginning to end on the DVD.

Selecting Additional Computer Hard Drives

Video consumes an enormous amount of hard drive storage space, approximately 230 MB per minute of video. Additional hard drive space of more than double that amount is needed during editing for transitions, effects, additional sound tracks, and exporting movies in distribution format. With these additional requirements for storage space, an extra hard drive is recommended.

External Firewire hard drives are the easiest way to add hard drive space to a computer. Portability of external drives is an asset when a project is completed. The user

Tip

Using network storage space for video is generally a bad idea. Moving the amount of data required for video over a network will severely strain the average school network and will usually give unsatisfactory results.

can plug the drive with the finished product into the computer that has the DVD burner on it and burn the project onto DVD.

Internal hard drives are less expensive than external drives because the manufacturer does not have to build an external case or a power supply. However, installing an internal drive is more complicated than installing a Firewire drive. Regardless of the type of hard drive selected, the additional drive will need to be at least a 7,200 rpm (rotations per minute) drive or faster.

Summary:

While the consumer market gradually converts from analog video to digital video, educators will need to work with both formats and help students convert their video projects to the format used in their homes. A basic understanding of the development of home video equipment, the hardware necessary to convert analog to digital, and digital compression, is the foundation of video-editing skills. With limited resources available for educators, wise selections of video hardware products are critical in order for students to obtain maximum quality in student-produced videos.

Chapter 3

Selecting Editing Software

Choosing Video-Editing Software

If a school is just starting out in digital video, or even if they have many seasoned videographers, the vast range of video-editing software products available may be overwhelming. Some of the higher end video-editing software packages cost $500 or more, while others are less than $100.

Price is often the first thing to consider when purchasing a video-editing package. Many like the powerful video-editing software, but for the average user, it is overkill unless there is direct classroom teaching on the use of the software. The cheaper video-editing software packages save money and can easily meet most of a school's video-editing needs. The school can always upgrade later.

Video file import and export capabilities are also of vital importance when considering video-editing software. Will there be a need to import QuickTime movie files or RealMedia video? If so, check the software package box for the import formats. The same is true for export to distribution formats. If Windows Media will be the main distribution format, will the software support that feature?

Will special effects be used extensively? Less expensive packages come with "stock" special effects that cannot be customized while the higher-level video-editing programs allow for flexibility with special effects.

Another consideration in purchasing video-editing software is whether it comes bundled with other software such as VCD/DVD authoring packages or music creation packages. The additional video and audio editing "suites" can save hundreds of dollars from what they would be if they were purchased separately.

Basic Features of Editing Software

A key component of a video-editing system is the software. Raw video footage can be played back on a television, but it will contain many dead moments that will detract from the video's highlights. Therefore, video-editing software is needed to remove non-essential clips and rearrange the video to best present its message. A multitude of editing tools such as additional audio tracks, still images, text, and transitions are included with each video-editing software package to create interest in the video. The primary difference between video-editing software is the level of sophistication of the additional editing tools.

In selecting a video-editing program, consideration of the display view should be one of the first issues considered. It is advisable to have both a storyboard and a timeline view available for use at different times during the video production. In a storyboard view, a small thumbnail picture represents each segment of video or image file.

A timeline view is necessary for isolating a small segment of video to be edited or eliminated. In a timeline view, video length is displayed, making it easy to move from the beginning or end of the clip. Some software packages allow the user to drag the end of a video clip toward a specific time marker on the timeline. A timeline view is essential for managing multiple video and audio tracks. The user has individual control over each track to add special effects.

Switching between storyboard and timeline view does not change the project, only the view of the project. The storyboard mode is used to view all the project clips at a glance, note the sequence, and drag clips to a new location within the project. The timeline view is used to trim clips, cut segments, and reposition audio and video track starting points.

Video-Editing Software Programs for the Mac

Since 2000, every new Mac has come with *iMovie* preinstalled in the application folder of the hard drive along with an *iMovie* CD. *iMovie* is also included with Mac OS X. Since the initial version of *iMovie*, the Apple Web site <www.apple.com/ilife/imovie/> has provided regular upgrades.

Although simple in design and interface, *iMovie* allows very sophisticated, professional-looking videos. With *iMovie 4*, users can quickly edit and trim right in the timeline by simply clicking and dragging. Audio and video can be synchronized with "snap to" precision.

iMovie is now included in *iLife '04*, which incorporates software for digital music, photography, moviemaking, and DVD creation. *iLive '04* is a suite of tightly integrated tools that work together seamlessly. Songs can be created in *GarageBand* and then saved automatically in *iTunes* where a user can easily access it when music is needed to accompany the *iPhoto* slide shows, to underscore the action in an *iMovie* project, or to play behind the titles of an *iDVD* project. *iLive '04* can be downloaded from <www.apple.com/ilife/> on the Apple Web site.

More advanced students and professionals working on a Mac operating system often purchase *Final Cut Pro*, which works in virtually any format, frame rate, and resolution. *Final Cut Pro 4* gives digital artists the freedom to explore their creativity, but its advantages must be weighed against the higher cost.

Video-Editing Software Programs for the PC

Just as the Mac OS X comes bundled with a video-editing software program, Windows XP comes bundled with Microsoft *Movie Maker 2*. *Movie Maker* users can import video clips from analog or digital video cameras and choose from more than 130 video effects, titles, and transitions. *Movie Maker 2* also includes an AutoMovie feature that will analyze the clips and music, and automatically generate a three- to five-minute film.

Windows *Movie Maker 2* <www.microsoft.com/windowsxp/moviemaker/default.asp> works with Windows Media Video 9 (part of Media Player 9 series) compresses the source video into a format that is 1/20th the size of an .avi file. This compression allows far more raw footage to be uploaded onto the hard drive, eliminating problems resulting from insufficient storage space for longer projects. This compressed format can easily be burned to CD, sent via e-mail to friends and relatives, or even transferred to a Pocket PC for playback.

Pinnacle Studio 9 is the most powerful, easy-to-use software video editor in the under $100 class. A user can capture home movies onto the computer, edit them, add titles, music, narration, and special effects, and then output the edited masterpiece to videotape, DVD, and the Internet in three basic steps.

Pinnacle Studio <www.pinnaclesys.com/ProductPage_n.asp?Product_ID=1501&Langue_ID=7> has been extremely popular in the K-12 environment, and the latest version of *Pinnacle Studio* is even easier to use, less crash prone, and contains many more features than previous versions. Its new features include native 16" by 9" (widescreen) support, third party plug-in support, automated editing, and audio- and video-correction tools.

Roxio *VideoWave Movie Creator* <www.roxio.com/en/products/videowave_movie_creator/index.jhtml> makes it easy to go from video camera all the way to DVD for under $50. It is an excellent software package for the value and includes an Automovie feature similar to the one in *Movie Maker 2*. With *VideoWave*, one can easily capture video from analog or digital sources and advance from automatic or guided editing to precision editing with easy-to-use tools. After editing, the user can drag and drop video clips into DVD menu templates and go directly to selected scenes using on-screen menu buttons and then burn the movies to CD or DVD.

Ulead *MediaStudio Pro 7* <www.ulead.com/msp/> is a complete digital video suite, offering Real-time MPEG capture, Real-time preview, as well as Real-time output. The suite includes tools for video painting, CG graphics, audio editing, and DVD authoring for broadcast, tape, DVD, or the Web. Ulead *Media Studio Pro* costs around $500.

Adobe *Premiere* is often considered the de facto standard for PC video-editing software programs. It is known for its exceptional editing power, speed, and control. Real-time editing enables the user to quickly create rough cuts for review and fine-tune productions before exporting. Professional editing tools provide precision in color correction, multiple timelines, digital effects, and much more. Powerful sample-level audio editing provides precise control over sound, and advanced controls let users create complex audio tracks such as 5.1 surround sound. Extensive hardware support and an open architecture provide the flexibility to work with virtually any format. Adobe *Premiere Pro* < http://store.adobe.com/products/premiere/> includes a huge variety of plug-ins on the Web, free online training, and certification.

In selecting video-editing software, sometimes the driest information is the most important. Reading product specifications definitely can be boring, but a user needs to know what the manufacturer says about the product without the marketing publicity that is found in their advertisements. The product specifications provide the requirements for the software and the video formats the program uses along with a list of editing tools and features that come with the application. Time spent in researching different features included in several software packages is well worth the time and can prevent a misguided financial investment.

Audio-Editing Software

The human ear makes allowances for imperfections in sound. Even though the mind can fabricate what is missing in a reproduction, the human mind can also reject what is incorrectly reproduced. People are intolerant of recorded voices that contain unnatural *sibilants* (hissing sounds) and sounds with clipped high notes or overly strong deep resonance, known as *distortion*.

Two kinds of distortion threaten the quality of audio reproduction, distortions caused by limitations of the recording device, and distortions caused by misuse of the recording device. There may be little that can be done about the limitations of the recording device, but proper instruction and care can cut down on the distortion caused by misuse.

Digitized sound is actually composed of sequences of individual sound samples. The number of samples per second is called the *sample rate* and is very much like a video track's *frame rate*. The more sound samples per second, the higher the quality of the resulting sound and the more storage space it requires.

Another property of a sound track is the number of channels it contains: one (mono) or two (stereo). Like video software, users can compress sound using techniques designed to represent the sound data more efficiently and to lower the data rate. Most digital video-editing software contains its own audio editing component, but occasionally people may confront a situation in which the audio needs to be edited in isolation.

GoldWave <www.goldwave.ca/> is one of the most complete, inexpensive audio-editing products for Windows. *GoldWave* contains basic audio editing features of fade, equalizer, doppler, mechanize, echo, reverse, and more advanced features (such as batch processor/converter, CD reader, and audio restoration filters) that cost extra in other, more expensive audio-editing programs. *GoldWave* is available for approximately $43.

In August 2003, Adobe released a repackaged version of *Cool Edit Pro 2.1* naming it *Adobe Audition*. *Adobe Audition* software <www.adobe.com/products/audition/main.html> is a professional audio-editing environment. *Adobe Audition* offers advanced audio mixing, editing, and effects-processing capabilities. Its flexible workflow coupled with exceptional ease of use and precise tools, provides the power to create rich, nuanced audio of the highest possible quality. *Adobe Audition* sells for approximately $299.

Smart Sound Movie Maestro <http://www.smartsound.com/moviemaestro/index.html> is a music software package designed for home video enthusiasts and educators to customize music soundtracks for any video project. *SmartSound Movie Maestro* music and the Movie Music series of CDs are licensed for non-commercial and educational use only.

For those who would like to test an audio editor without investing capital, there is a free download, *Audacity* <http://audacity.sourceforge.net/>. A user can record and play sounds, import and export WAV, AIFF, Ogg Vorbis, MP3 files, and more. One can edit sounds using Cut, Copy, and Paste (with unlimited Undo), mix tracks together, or apply effects to the recordings. *Audacity* also has a built-in amplitude envelope editor, a customizable spectrogram mode, and a frequency analysis window for audio analysis applications. This free audio editor also includes built-in effects of Echo, Change Tempo, and Noise Removal.

Summary:

Cost should never be the primary consideration for the selection of a video-editing software package. Individual features of each software package need to be compared with the previous training of the students and the instructional objectives of the educator before the final selection of video- and audio-editing software is made. Only after consulting several professional reviews should a purchase of a major video product be made.

Chapter 4

Organizing a School

Media Production Area

Setting up a School Video Studio

When setting up a school video studio, library media specialists and teachers need first to consider the physical space available. School video studios range from a temporary section in the library media center to a multiple-room production suite. Whether a permanent set is used or a portable space that must be shared with other activities, to save frustrations, all equipment and supplies must be kept in its place. Since it takes a great deal of time and effort to set up the studio, it is ideal if the equipment is not taken to other parts of the building later in the day. Changing cable setup can cause unbelievable headaches.

If possible, a permanent studio of 18 feet by 16 feet would be ideal and would provide the flexibility necessary for preparing a wide variety of school video productions. While space is an essential consideration, so are temperature and humidity. Computers, video equipment, and tapes are sensitive to temperature and moisture. An air-conditioned environment of a constant 72 degrees is recommended.

Whatever the size, a vital rule in arranging a set is to keep it simple. The viewers should not be distracted with unnecessary items. At the same time, there should be no empty spots. The most important consideration in developing a set is to concentrate on only what the camera will see. The talent and simple unobtrusive decoration should fill the screen.

The two basic designs for a set for a school video studio include the standard news show and the informal talk show set, which includes office or reception area chairs placed close together in a living room style. If possible, the set needs to be placed on a platform approximately two feet tall, five to six feet long and four to five feet wide. The platform will allow normal camera operation while eliminating a downward tilt of the camera and keep the cameraperson from having to bend over constantly. The platform also allows for better angle shots with most of those shots being at eye-level.

Backdrop

The background of a set should be subtle and unobtrusive, yet not bland. The backdrop should be at least 10 feet high and 13 feet wide. A drop cloth or two king-size bed sheets painted with latex water-based, light colored paint can serve as an inexpensive backdrop. If possible, the tiles in the ceiling could be removed; holes could be punched in the sheet or drop cloth and tied with string to the support beam above the tile.

For a more professional-looking set, a "flat" can be placed in the back of the set. A flat is a background that covers the area in the back of where the talent sits. It consists of a wooden frame approximately seven feet high by 15 feet wide covered with a muslin cloth or canvas. The canvas or muslin is stretched over the frame as tightly as possible and attached with nails or a staple gun. Students can create their own flat by covering the flat with latex paint with a roller and then painting it with their desired color or design.

Chroma Key (a.k.a. chromakey)

With the advent of digital video-editing, students are now able to use Chroma Key (a.k.a. chromakey) in their own video productions. This same effect is used on the weather news when the anchor stands in front of a blank green or blue panel and points while a map digitally replaces the green or blue panel.

With updated technology, Chroma Key is not limited to the professionals, but can easily be duplicated in schools across the country. One way to do this is by painting a section of the wall in a video studio with Rosco Blue or Green DigiComp Paint for Chroma Key and Blue Screen use. After the video clip is imported into the computer, the video technicians can place the desired background in the second timeline video track.

A less expensive way to achieve the Chroma Key effect is to use Chroma Key Blue (or Green) Screen Foam Backed Fabric, which is sold as a bolt 60 inches wide and 40 yards long for less than $20. The felt-like fabric is specially designed for blue screen work. It absorbs light and has low reflectance qualities. The foam-backed Chroma key fabric also has the ability to be stretched and can be pulled tight on homemade frames to help resist wrinkles, the number one enemy of successful and evenly lit composite work.

For a more sophisticated use of the Chroma Key effect, 10 foot by 30 foot Chroma Key Green or Blue Screen Fabric is available for less than $300. It is made from a cotton-like material without a foam background so it has the flexibility to cover almost any item or part of a human body and can be replaced with a multitude of digital effects. This method is common in many science fiction movies.

By using Chroma Key products, students can create many of the effects they see on television or the movies and develop a greater understanding of media literacy and how easily media can be distorted to persuade or influence the viewer. These items can be obtained through online stores such as <http://filmtools.com/> that provide supplies for film and video professionals.

To add an even more exciting set, virtual backgrounds to use with Chroma Key are available from such vendors as <http://www.simpleset.com/>. Virtual sets provide an inexpensive source for moving graphics that would not be possible at most schools. With a virtual background, students will be able to proceed normally with their TV production's regular movement and rhythm. The talent can walk around the Chroma Key blue stage freely in the midst of virtual objects.

Acoustics

The best location of a school TV studio is often dependent on the acoustics of the area. Sound is more affected by the acoustics of a room or studio than most people realize. When setting up a video studio, whether it is temporary or permanent, the acoustics of the area must be given careful consideration. Some of the sound waves need to be absorbed by objects in the room and some need to be scattered, for a sound source to sound "real."

Sound is scattered by the metal and plastic in TV studio equipment and bounces back from the floor and the cinderblocks in the walls or tiles. A cloth backdrop is an excellent source for absorbing those random sound waves. Other good sources for absorbing sound waves are a rug and chairs made with fabric.

To obtain optimum acoustics in the school video studio, students can experiment by adding or taking away more fabric elements such as cloth backdrops or padded chairs. The goal is for the sound to seem natural. With too much fabric, the sound will seem dead and with too many hard surfaces, the sound will seem like it needs less treble and more bass. Sometimes carpet blocks can be used on part of the cinderblock walls for better acoustics.

Lighting

The most common solution for picture quality problems is to control the light. In a school video studio, the lighting can be as simple as using natural light or the light on the camcorder. However, the most common lighting configuration is three-point lighting, which can be as simple as 250-300 watt clip-on lights or lights with stands.

The first light, called a *key light*, covers the left-hand side of the subject's face. The key light is commonly located about 45 degrees to the right or left of the camera.

The second light, the *fill light*, is softer and fills the shadows created by the first light. It is commonly located 30 to 45 degrees from the camera, opposite the key, and at the same height.

A third light, *back light or kicker light*, is used to create a feeling of depth.

The *back light* is placed behind the talent near ground level, and pointed upward, slightly toward the background. This light helps decrease the shadow caused by the key light, create visual separation between the subject and the background. The back light can be used to create interest in the backdrop, create a halo of light on the hair and shoulders of the talent, or on the top of objects being video taped. Like the key and fill light, it should be on as close to a direct line with the camera as is practical.

Figure 4:1 Light Setup

Variations in three-point lighting can include removing ceiling tiles to allow the lights to be higher so they can shoot at a downward angle, eliminating shadows. Ambient lighting can be used as a fill light, if the window is in the right location, but in order to obtain the best quality, the correct angle needs to be maintained.

Some student video studios include a light board and dimmers. A light switcher board is comparable to an audio mixer. A series of fader bars allows combinations of several different studio lights while the dimmers control the lights.

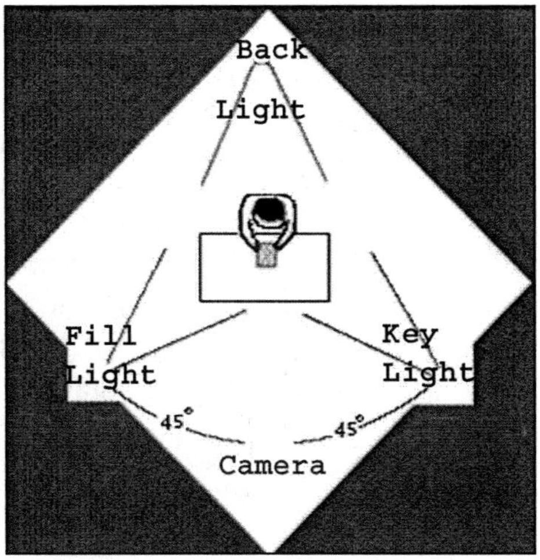

Equipment

The basic single camera configuration used in most school video studios includes six critical items: a camcorder, a power supply, a tripod, a microphone, a headset, and a stop watch or clock. Variations of the basic configuration may vary according to the local budget and the audio/video needs of the school. Creativity can often over-compensate for minimal equipment, and students can prepare quality productions in spite of limited funding.

An audience will be more forgiving of bad shots than they will be of faulty audio. While the on-camera microphone will suffice for minimal quality audio, an external microphone provides clarity and eliminates static from the camcorder motor. A cordless microphone, consisting of two transmitters and one receiver, is an affordable solution to this problem. The receiver fits on top of the camcorder and replaces the camcorder's built-in microphone. A handheld microphone and a lavaliere microphone (one worn around the neck or clipped to a lapel) are used in an interview situation while co-anchors need two lavalieres.

Regardless of the microphone system, the director must communicate with camera operators or talent with hand signals because the microphone would pick up voices. Many television personalities and politicians have been embarrassed when their spoken comments were picked up while they thought the microphones had been turned off.

In a more sophisticated school media environment, a multiple-camera configuration can be utilized for remote broadcasts of awards assemblies, pep rallies, school plays, or a large video production room. In a typical multi-camera unit, the users can operate up to four cameras from one multiple-camera setup. The camera's directional antennas must point in the same general direction so that they may utilize the same receiver and maintain consistent audio.

Whether in a studio or on location, whenever possible, a tripod is necessary to provide stability for the video. To add a more professional look, wheels can be added to the tripod, which changes it into a dolly. A tripod and removable wheels cost about $400. The word *dolly* not only refers to the wheel attachment, but also to the forward or backward movement of the camera on the tripod.

Regardless of the studio or an on-site location shoot, the source of camera power is critical. The power supply for portable video equipment can be either *alternating current* (AC) found in all outlets or *direct current* (DC) found in batteries. If a person is videotaping within a reasonable distance of a wall electrical plug, the AC should be used so that the user will not have to worry about the battery running out at a crucial point in the video program. The circumstances of the videotaping assignment dictate the power source.

Setting up a Media Production Room

If space is available, it is best to have a separate room from the video studio as a media production or control room. A media production room needs to be adjacent to the video studio and at least eight feet deep by 18 feet long and eight feet high. It is preferred that the window between the control room and the floor of the studio be at least three feet high and 11 feet long.

The center of a production-room computer system could include audio- and video-editing software, a CD or DVD burner, a capture card, speakers, an external hard drive, a good audio card with both analog and digital inputs and outputs, Internet connection, a microphone, and headphones. A device to convert computer signal to analog is helpful so PowerPoint or HyperStudio slides can be recorded on a VCR and shown on the student-produced TV show.

Two separate VCRs and dual monitors for dubbing are common in a basic media production environment. It must be remembered that each time an analog videotape is copied, a generation is lost and the video quality drops dramatically.

In a more sophisticated media production environment, a video switcher can be a valuable tool. Two or more cameras can be connected to a switcher in a multiple camera configuration. By pushing a button or operating a fader bar, a video source is selected or modified, and then out putted into a single video. With the multiple-camera configuration, the final audio and video signals are not recorded by the camcorders but on a separate videotape recorder. The main switcher output and the main audio output are connected as inputs to the recording VCR.

When using a video switcher, a monitor is needed for each video input along with a separate one for the final lineout video that carries the final video picture.

Audio-Mixing Console

An audio mixer is vital to balance the sound between the live microphone inputs, background music, and the videotaped line inputs. The mixer lets the technician hear the sources both before and after they are selected by monitoring the audio through headphones and speakers.

In a complex video studio, an intercom system (headset and wall-mount) can provide communications between studio and production room. A headset system enables the technical director in the control room to talk to the director, floor director, and camera operators in the studio. A wall-mounted intercom between the control room and the video studio is used when the director needs to speak with the entire crew, including talent, at the same time.

Volume Unit (VU) Meter Settings

Figure 4.2: Audio Mixer

A *VU meter* shows the audio technician the level or intensity of the sound entering the audio mixer. A VU meter is usually labeled -20 to +3. The zero represents 100 percent of the mixer's capability. Most meters print the area over the zero in red ink, and the lower, acceptable level in black. A good rule is "the level should approach the red, but not go into it."

The technician should keep the VU meter level below the zero level (100 percent). If the meter gives a higher reading, the audio will become fuzzy and unclear. If the VU meter does not move toward the 100 percent mark occasionally, the input is set too low, and the sound will be thin, and weak, not rich and full.

Adjusting a VU meter is simple. The audio technician wears a headphone plugged into the headphone jack of the audio mixer. As the CD is playing, the technician adjusts the fader to the correct level. At the same time, the microphone input fader is adjusted so the voice dominates as the music provides a pleasant background. The master output controls the intensity of the final mix produced by the audio mixer.

Media Distribution Unit

For maximum flexibility, include the media distribution unit, or Channel One Head Unit, in the media production area. With this configuration, the camcorder can be attached directly to the head unit and news shows can be broadcasted live, if the VCRs are set to Line or AUX position. The distribution head unit needs to be strategically placed since the audio and video quality is diminished if the RCA cables are too long.

Summary:

A school video studio and media production rooms can provide students with a realistic environment to help them master a multitude of skills and standards. Not only is a better understanding of media and visual literacy achieved, but technical skills are increased as well. Being able to appear before the camera increases a student's self-confidence as she receives admiration from classmates. However, one of the most important advantages of participating in a school video production program is the ability to collaborate with others and observe the importance of the behind-the-scenes crew in a television or video production.

Chapter

Pre-Production

Pre-Production Checklist

The quality of an audio/video project is directly proportional to the time spent in pre-production and storyboarding. The most important step in pre-production is to identify clearly the goals and purposes of the production. Before starting, the audio/video equipment needs to be checked and instruction given as to the use and care of the equipment before production begins. The props, personnel, and location of shooting need to be arranged, necessary releases and permissions obtained, and a storyboard prepared before starting to videotape. Detailed planning will eliminate a great deal of frustrations later.

The easiest and best way to prepare a class video is to follow a consistent checklist such as the one in Figure 5.1.

Storyboards and Scripts

Storyboards are designed to be a rough approximation of what will be produced. Storyboards consist of drawings of key scenes with corresponding notes on dialogue, sound effects, music, and special effects. One of the first steps in preparing a storyboard is to determine the type of show being produced. There are semi-scripted shows and fully-scripted shows.

In the first category are interviews, discussions, ad-lib shows, demonstrations, and variety shows. The scripts for semi-scripted shows often resemble a basic outline, with only the show segments and their times indicated on the script.

A fully-scripted video needs a more detailed storyboard that includes a sketch of the video of each scene, narration, music or other audio background, size, color, and placement of graphics, the actual text, along with its color, size and text, and audience interaction, and anything else the production crew needs to know.

Quality storyboards can be achieved in several methods. Storyboards can be sketched by hand by using a template similar to the one in Figure 5.2. The important part of the hand-drawn storyboard is not the artwork, but the thought process involved.

Sample Pre-Production Checklist

Date Completed	Tasks	Details
	Purpose of Video Identified	
	Intended Audience Identified	
	Summary Paragraph	
	Equipment Needed	
	Props Needed	
	Location(s) Identified	
	Talent(s) Identified	
	Storyboard Drafted or Narrative Written	
	Required Graphics, Photos, Audio or Video Clips Gathered	
	Necessary Copyright, Permissions and Clearances Obtained	
	Production Schedule Prepared	

Storyboard Template

Frame #	Frame #	Frame #
Video Sketch	Video Sketch	Video Sketch
Type of Camera Shot (Close Up)	Type of Camera Shot (Medium)	Type of Camera Shot (Distant)
Narration	Narration	Narration
Background Audio	Background Audio	Background Audio
Overlaying Text or Graphics	Overlaying Text or Graphics	Overlaying Text or Graphics

Many software packages can be used to prepare storyboards. A video producer can create a storyboard using the drawing tools in Microsoft *Word* or first create the storyboard as an organizational chart in Microsoft *Word* and then save it or copy it into a Web page. Similar tools are also available in *PowerPoint* and Microsoft *Publisher*.

The concept mapping software, *Inspiration*, <http://www.inspiration.com/home.cfm> is often used in schools to prepare storyboards. This software provides an opportunity for students to express themselves visually and to recognize the connection between words and meanings. The flexibility of *Inspiration* makes it an excellent selection to help students think through the video-making process.

Figure 5.3: Storyboard Screenshot

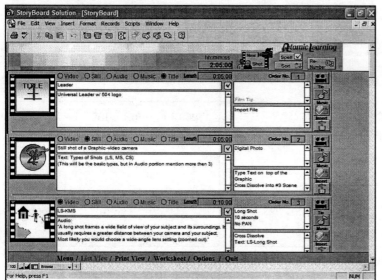

Several software packages are designed specifically for storyboard preparation. One popular free storyboard-preparation package is *Atomic Learning's FREE Video StoryBoard Pro* <http://www.atomiclearning.com/storyboardpro> designed for teachers, students, and home moviemakers as a tool in creating video projects. With students' fast acceptance of new technologies, an online storyboard may encourage more preplanning than they normally would do by making crude sketches.

Kids Video <http://kidsvid.hprtec.org/ scripting.html> has prepared an online storyboard to help younger students visualize movie ideas. These storyboards provide a step-by-step approach for students to understand the many details that must blend in order to produce a video.

Obtaining Taping Permission for Individual Students

Child safety and security is a primary concern of educators and parents. All precautions need to be taken to protect children while providing them with the educational richness obtained in video production. Most schools have a specific policy pertaining to the release of student images. However, many parents sign school release forms without spending time considering their content and may need to be reminded of their signature when a privacy issue arises.

If a student's image is to be used beyond the confines of the classroom, specific permission should be obtained from each parent. If a school has not adopted a district-wide form, the individual library media specialist or teacher may need to develop their own form.

Parental permission forms for using students in videos should include:

- the name of the video project
- the dates of production
- the purpose of the project
- names of those involved in producing the video
- location or setting of the video footage
- how talent will be identified in the video

- the intended audience
- method of duplication or distribution (if applicable)
- how the parents may access or preview the completed video

Special precautions need to be taken when videotaping students with Individual Educational Plans (IEPs). If the student with an IEP is in a group setting within the special education room, videotaping her image is covered under the same guidelines as other students in the school. The Family Educational Rights and Privacy Act (FERPA) 20 U.S.C. § 1232, 34 C.F.R. § 99 and the Individuals with Disabilities Education Act (IDEA) require that students should not be videotaped in any location, such as the special education classroom, that identifies a particular student as a student in need of assistance. Before a video-recording device is used to tape a student in need of special assistance, the IEP team should review the purpose of the recording and the parents should sign a permission form.

Obtaining Taping Permission for Locations

In most situations, not only will permission for videotaping students need to be obtained, but also permission to use a particular site must be obtained if an off-campus location is selected. If private property will be used, a written agreement needs to be signed by those involved.

It can no longer be assumed that if a videographer is on public property, he does not need to ask permission to videotape on that site. Most colleges and universities have a strict procedure policy to follow before videotaping on campus. To receive permission to videotape on campus, school officials should first consider the impact the video project would have on class schedules, the interruption of student learning, and ease of movement around campus.

When videotaping on a city street, it is best to have a signed release from any business whose sign may be in the background of a shoot. An explanation and an agreement between the videographer and the business owner needs to include the impact of interruption of normal activities in the area during the shooting of the video along with where and how the video will be distributed.

After the events of Sept. 11, 2001 and the creation of The Department of Homeland Security, greater precautions must be taken before videotaping in a public area. Local law enforcement may need to be contacted as to the videotaping policies in any given location. For example, the Port Authority reserves the right to restrict videotaping and photography at its airports. Videotaping in runway and taxiway areas at all airports is prohibited at all times. Videotaping around the toll plazas of bridges and tunnels under the control of the Port Authority is also restricted.

Homeland Security officials are training local citizens to be vigilant in reporting those videotaping in unusual circumstances. Therefore, it is best to alert the local law enforcement well in advance of any major outdoor film shoot to avoid delays that may occur while the purpose of a video project is being verified.

Agreements between property owner and video producer should include: the name of the video project, the dates of production, the purpose of the project, names of those involved in producing the video, the intended audience, location or setting of the video footage, explanation of any interruption of normal use of property while the video is being shot (if applicable), guarantee of the return of property to the same condition as when film crew arrived, method of duplication or distribution (if applicable), and signatures of property owners and those responsible for the video production.

Preparing and Organizing Students as Videographers

One of the first challenges student videographers face is to understand the difference between video production and public speaking. Video productions require more visual stimulation. The video audiences are accustomed to a steady stream of visual stimulus and are quickly bored with talking heads.

Viewers even become restless with a steady stream of still images. To provide visual stimulation to a still image on a video, video producers can now pan over the pictures or fade them in and out at various locations in the picture. (This is a technique perfected by Ken Burns in his PBS series of historical documentaries.)

Preparing a group video helps students develop collaboration and problem solving skills. Each participant needs to be aware of not only his responsibility in the production, but also the role of each of the other members in the production crew. Defining each person's position will prevent later conflicts. As crew members understand the responsibilities of their particular position, they will be less likely to try to interject their personal perception into a production in areas in which they are unfamiliar or pull back if the production does not go their way. While work assignments may vary from project to project, the basic positions include:

- Producer—implements the program concept, lays out the timetable, and keeps the project on task.

- Talent—refers to anyone whose voice is heard or who appears on camera.

- Camera operator—does more than just operate the camera; he sets up the cameras and ensures technical quality. The camera operator works with the director, lighting director, and audio technician in setting up and shooting every scene. On a field production, he arranges for camera equipment pickup and delivery.

- Director—is in charge of the pre-production details, coordinating the activities of the production staff and talent, selecting camera shots during production, and supervising post-production work.

- Technical director—is responsible for the technical aspects of the production.

Summary:

The more time a student spends in the pre-production stage, the more time will be saved during the production period and the better the quality of the final product. The more detailed the storyboard, the easier the shooting and editing processing. Detailed group planning is critical at the pre-production stage of development. One of the greatest values gained in working on a video production crew is the ability to collaborate with fellow students.

Chapter 6

Selecting Distribution Formats

Choosing Platforms and File Formats

The main advantage of using digital is that once a file is in a digital format, it can be easily displayed and distributed in several different media forms. Before beginning to edit a digital video, the video producer needs to consider how the video will be distributed since distribution formats will affect the settings used when first opening a video-editing program. Although many digital videos are currently being copied onto an analog VHS tape for distribution, it is now becoming more common to distribute digital video on CD or DVD discs or over the Internet.

The final format of a video not only determines the compression used in editing digital video, but it also affects the techniques used in shooting the video. Occasionally a person may choose to distribute their digital video in several different formats so modifications will need to be made early in the production process.

The advantages of using digital media as the distribution format include not only high video resolution and sound fidelity, 4.7 gigabytes of storage capacity, but also the ability to author the DVD in a menu format. With a DVD menu format, viewers can go directly to the particular clip that interests them, while they would need to spend time fast-forwarding a VCR tape to a specific spot. Using the DVD format, students can include a digital photo album as well as the video itself. DVD producers can include a folder of digital images and create a slide show of interesting but unused photos. To add even more interest to a slideshow, a soundtrack can be added.

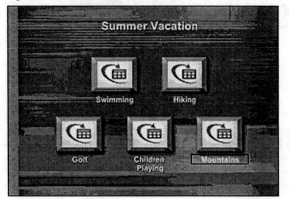

When DVD players become the standard household video devices, DVD will be the ideal distribution format. However, since we are in a transition period from analog to digital, the availability of technology in the viewers' homes should be one of the primary considerations of the final format of a class video. Schools will need to provide student videos in several different formats until the transfer to all-digital video is complete.

Transferring Your Desktop onto a VHS Tape

There are situations when educators may need to make a videotape recording of a *PowerPoint* presentation or record a tutorial in VHS format. Unfortunately, televisions are still primitive compared to computer monitors. Even high-quality televisions with high vertical and horizontal resolutions may have problems displaying a computer image, due to limitations in the way video signals are encoded. The maximum resolution that a television will display is probably less than 640 by 480, a very low desktop resolution for a PC. VHS videotapes are even more limited.

If a person plans to record a presentation such as *PowerPoint* or *HyperStudio* to videotape, they must use a low desktop resolution and big fonts. Where possible, S-video connectors instead of standard RCA video plugs should be used.

Figure 6.2: Scan Converter

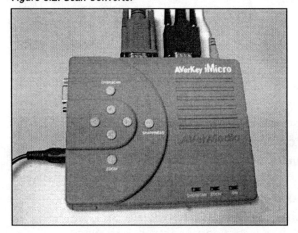

The easiest way to add TV output to a computer system is to add a *scan converter*—an external box that takes the PC digital video signal and converts it to an NTSC video signal used by televisions and VCRs. Most scan converters have both standard RCA-plug outputs and S-video outputs. They work with any computers and operating systems that support standard PC monitor outputs, including PC desktops, Macs, and laptops.

A basic scan converter costs around $90. Higher-cost scan converters add features like zoom and pan, and often have higher quality signal electronics for a slightly better picture. If a scan converter is to be installed in a video production or projection facility, a high-end rack mounted scan converter that converts several inputs and allows easy switching between devices can be purchased.

If upgrading a computer, a school may want to select a video card that supports TV Out along with Video In. TV Out cards allow the users to connect an RCA plug or S-video connector directly to the video card, for easy video output to a TV or VCR.

Transferring Video to CD-ROM

Video CD, or VCD, is a primitive version of DVD. It is a kind of CD and looks the same as a music CD or a CD-ROM, except instead of music or software it holds movies. Video CD uses MPEG-1 video compression to achieve approximately 74 minutes of video. Its resolution is 352 by 240 (NTSC) or 352 by 288 (PAL), which is roughly comparable to VHS.

Most, but not all, DVD players will play back VCD. CDs need to be properly written to CD-R; otherwise, a VCD-compatible DVD player will not be able to read them properly. Most CD burning programs have a VCD template, which ensures a properly written VCD. The main advantage of video CD versus DVD is that it is relatively easy to create video CDs using a CD-ROM burner.

One-step up from MPEG-1 format used in Video CDs is MPEG-2 with 720 by 480 resolution and 60 fields per second. The video portion of DVD-Video is MPEG-2. The DVD format also supports Dolby AC-3 audio, multiple audio tracks, navigable menus, and several other features.

Video Conversion

Many school and home libraries are in the process of converting their video libraries from analog to digital. Before changing format of a commercial videotape, copyright clearance will need to be obtained; while formats of home and school- produced videos can be transferred at the owner's discretion.

Several companies have developed products that capture analog video and convert them to the digital format using only a USB connection. Many schools choose this method of conversion because they will most likely not have to upgrade their computer and will not have to open the computer to install a Firewire card. The major drawback of these devices is the quality of the video captured. A person cannot send full-format digital video files (720 by 480 pixels, 29.97 frames per second) over a USB 1.1 cable because the bandwidth restriction will cause dropped frames during capture. USB connectors work well for a smaller format video of 352 by 288 pixels or smaller and work well if the desired output is Web video or CD-ROM.

A better way to convert analog video to digital video is to purchase internal computer cards that have S-video or A/V jacks on them. These conversion devices are to video as modems are to telecommunications. In telecommunications, modems convert the signal from analog (phone lines) to digital bits so the computer can process the files for communication. Likewise, video conversion devices convert analog video signals from a VHS, Hi-8, or VHS-S camera and turn them into digital files that the video-editing software will be able to recognize.

How to Convert VHS Tapes to DVDs

To convert a VHS tape to DVD, a DVD writer, a video-capture card, and the appropriate drivers and software should first be installed. Connect a VCR or camcorder to the analog-in ports on the video capture device and select a video source within the recording software (VHS tape or TV show or camcorder). The next step is to select the video quality (resolutions, frame sizes, frame rates, and bit rate) and record video to the computer hard drive. Edit the video, and author the DVD with the DVD program included with the DVD burner to create a menu and add videos. Last of all, burn the DVD.

How to Transfer Video from a Digital Video Camera to VHS Tape

1. Place DV tape into digital video camera.

2. Switch the camera mode to VTR.

3. Open the LCD panel on the side of the digital camcorder.

4. Rewind the tape.

5. Remove the "cap" on the digital camcorder covering several jacks.

6. Connect an S-video cable to the top jack labeled "S Video" and connect the other end to the S-video jack on the back of the VCR.

7. Connect a cable from the video-out on the back of the VCR to the video-in on the back of the monitor.

8. Connect an audio cable (has red and white jacks) from the audio-out on the VCR to the audio-in on the monitor (using only one of the colored ends on the monitor side is okay, red or white if there is only one audio-in hole).

9. Connect an audio cable with male 1/8-inch stereo RCA plug to the audio/video jack (just below the S-video slot) on the digital camcorder. At the other end of the cable, place each stereo plug into the audio-in jack, for audio transfer.

10. Place the VHS tape into the VCR.

11. Cue the VHS tape to the appropriate slot.

12. To start recording, press record on the VCR and play on the digital camcorder.

13. To test recording results—Stop the digital camcorder and the VCR, rewind the VCR to the place recording was started and press play.

Inserting Digital Video into PowerPoint Presentations

When inserting a video clip into a *PowerPoint* presentation (Insert->Movies and Sounds->Movie from File), the creator must decide if the movie will begin immediately when the slide is displayed or if the movie will start when the link is clicked. The movie will appear on the slide without a controller bar.

When creating a hyperlink to a movie (Insert->Hyperlink), the movie will launch in the default media player for the movie type (Windows Media Player, QuickTime Player, and Real Player). When the hyperlink (which can be a user created text or a button/icon) is clicked, the movie will appear in a separate window along with familiar controller options of the media player.

Generally, a QuickTime movie (.mov) cannot be inserted into Windows *PowerPoint*. A QuickTime movie (.mov) can be imported into Macintosh *PowerPoint*, but the movie probably will not play if on a presentation from a PC.

Windows Media files (.wmv) and MPEG files (.mpeg, .mpg) are good options to insert into Windows *PowerPoint* presentations. These file formats offer good quality video at small file sizes. Inserted Windows Media files (.wmv) will not play back with Macintosh *PowerPoint*, but MPEG files (.mpeg, .mpg) will. Thus, MPEG files (.mpeg, .mpg) are good choices for cross-platform presentations with inserted movies.

Transferring Video via the World Wide Web

A movie that does well on the Web will most often be short and to the point. Scenes may need to be cut and mainly close-ups of main subjects used. Showing panoramic, big spaces on Internet video usually does not work, since the picture can become fuzzy, jerky during playback, and take up more file space.

To create Web-based videos, reduce file size, frame rate, color, and audio depth. Make audio tracks mono. Use few colors, avoid transitions, and set the frame rate between six and 15 frames per second to reduce bandwidth.

Streaming video technology speeds delivery to the viewer. To create streaming media, the creator will need a video to convert the video into one of the three popular streaming formats: RealNetwork's RealVideo, Microsoft's Windows Media Technologies, and Apple's QuickTime. The viewer will need a player for the format of the video in order to view the video. These viewers are available as a free download from the manufacturers' Web sites.

Since the computer can often play back audio and video faster than it can be sent over the network, the streaming process is a way to give the playback a head start. The computer quietly receives and stores enough of a broadcast so it can keep up, and then begins playing that portion back while the rest of the data is received in the background.

To stream video so it plays in real-time requires trading off video quality for immediate playback. If a viewer is connected by modem, the producer can encode the video so it goes over that slow link, but the quality will be substantially degraded. If the producer assumes that the receiver is using better connections, they can encode the video so it is better, but the viewer with slower connections will not be able to view it.

A person can have high quality Internet video, or immediately accessible video, but not both. One way around this is to encode very short video clips at high data rates. The shortness of the clip keeps the file size manageable. Another advantage of short clips is that you can put them on your Web site without needing streaming media software on the server.

When QuickTime, Windows Media Player, or Real Player plays a video back, the clip is decompressed using the same codec in which it was compressed. Media players each recognize a different file format or extension (the letters to the right of the period in a file name). **.Mov** is recognized by QuickTime. Video for Windows, built into the Windows operating system, recognizes the **.avi** file extension.

Audio players include WinAmp, MusicMatch, and RealJukebox for PCs and Liquid Audio for MACs. Audio files on a MAC are generally **.aiff** files while audio files on a PC are generally **.wav**. The major audio codecs include MP3, WMA, Real Audio, and now MP3 Pro.

Video E-mail

Video files are usually too large for most people to send or receive, and, in any case, most people are cautious about opening e-mail attachments. Video e-mail is an e-mail message with a video file either inserted in the body of the message or accessible through a hypertext link.

There are a number of different approaches to video e-mail. One application, *Videogram Creator*, allows the sender to create a video message from previously recorded video data. The message is highly compressed into an HTML file that, at the receiving end, plays through a Java applet and looks like a Web page when opened.

VMdirect, a Las Vegas-based video e-mail company, takes a different approach. To use the VMdirect service, the sender records her message, which is then uploaded to the company's server. The recipient gets an e-mail message with a hyperlink to the file, which she can view online and download to save if she chooses.

Adapting Video for People with Disabilities

Technology has long been known as a vital assistant for people with disabilities; students can help prepare such videos for themselves and their classmates. Windows users could consider *Media Access Generator* (MAGpie), a caption-creation tool designed to make video materials more accessible to people with disabilities that is free from the National Center for Accessible Media.

Video on Pocket PCs

Pocket*TV* is the most downloaded third party Pocket PC and Smartphone application. Pocket*TV* can play any standard MPEG-1 video file (extension .mpg or .mpeg). Pocket*TV* is also capable of streaming MPEG video files using standard Internet protocols such as http, if the device has a wireless network connection that supports the necessary bandwidth of the MPEG file desired for streaming. The question remains: will watching video on a handheld computer become popular with the public?

Summary:

Several issues need to be considered when selecting a distribution format for a video. The final format of a video not only determines the compression used in the editing process, but it also affects the techniques used in shooting the video. The highest quality, most informative video is of little value if it is not in distribution formats available to the potential viewers. Often it is necessary to convert the same video into several different formats to accommodate the wide variety of consumer technology in use today.

Chapter

Understanding

Digital Compression

Fundamentals of Compression

Understanding digital compression is a difficult but critical aspect of digital editing. It is not necessary for the amateur video editor to memorize the ever-changing complexity of digital compression, but a basic understanding of types and uses of compression will prevent a great deal of lost time and frustration. Knowing the type of compression to be used in the final rendering of a video will affect not only how the video is shot, but also how it is edited.

Uncompressed, a single minute of video totals about 1GB while a three-minute song would occupy about 27 MB of file storage space. Clearly, uncompressed audio or video is not an option. Therefore, a codec, a short form for compression/decompression, must be used.

The final step in preparing a digital video clip is called *rendering,* which compresses the video using some form of codec. All good video capture programs contain several compression options before recording or importing video. Many video-editing software programs will assist users in selecting suitable compression formats by organizing templates according to the output desired. The software will automatically limit frame size, frame rate, and audio quality and provide other space-saving options. For example, if the user plans to distribute the movie as a VCD, the user can simply choose one of the VCD options, and the software will adjust the necessary settings.

Types of Video Codecs (COmpression/DECompression)

Compression works by eliminating unnecessary color information in a file, thus reducing the file size. A reduction of color also means diminished quality, depending on which compression scheme is chosen. Most video codecs consist of a *lossy* compression scheme in which digital information is lost during the compression process.

The two basic types of video compression are *interframe* and *intraframe*. *Interframe* compression compares consecutive frames of video, looking for frames where most of the pixels are not moving. If a person has a video clip of an animal running across the screen, most of the frame would remain unchanged, while only the part where the animal is actually in the frame would change. With interframe compression, the video would "recycle" the parts of the frames that are static background, and only refresh the parts of the frames where the animal actually moves across the screen.

Intraframe compression works on the premise that when the user knows that a pixel is going to be one color, she can assume that the pixels surrounding the pixel with known color are likely to be the same color. That way, the software only has to keep absolute tabs on a certain number of pixels, while letting the law of averages guess what color other pixels should be. Intraframe works well with solid colors, but has a hard time guessing when complex patterns are involved.

Video Compression Formats

For distributing video over a Web site or via e-mail, the most popular compression formats for Mac QuickTime files are Cinepak, Sorenson, and Sorenson3. QuickTime Version 6 and newer also includes MPEG-4 video compression, which provides an excellent balance of quality versus size for files being downloaded via the Web.

Indeo video compression was created by Intel and has been shipped with Windows since 1994 and with Apple's QuickTime since 1998, making it another of the widely available codecs. Indeo produces movies that are small enough for the Web, and look good on playback. Indeo is often used for quality AVI videos and movies that will be played back from a hard drive. Viewers must have the same version of Indeo compression for playback on their computers that corresponds with the version used to compress it. If the same version is not found, the viewer's movie play will attempt to establish an Internet connection and download the correct compression version, installing it as unobtrusively as possible.

MPEG (pronounced M-peg), which stands for "Moving Picture Experts Group", is the nickname given to a family of International Standards used for coding audio-visual information in a digital compressed format. The MPEG family of standards includes *MPEG-1*, *MPEG-2*, and *MPEG-4*. The MPG format frequently offers better compression along with better image and sound quality than the AVI format. MPG export is not supported as widely as AVI export, but most video editors can convert AVI files into MPG files.

MPEG-1 is the best MPEG Media Type for use on the Web and for use in videos that will be distributed via e-mail since files are generally easier on system resources and smaller in file size. An issue that must be considered when selecting an MPEG Media Type is the CPU speed of the system that will play the video. For example, even slightly older Pentium systems (such as those with CPU speeds under 350-450 MHz) cannot reliably decode and play the MPEG-2 media type. However, MPEG-1 can be decoded and played on just about any Pentium (or generic Pentium) computer.

NTSC VCD and *PAL VCD* are both variations on the MPEG 1 format that are used to create video compact disks that can be played back on televisions (by using a compatible DVD player). The NTSC standard is used in North America, while the PAL standard is used in Europe. Simply copying an MPG VCD file to a CD will not enable the file to be played back on a television unless the CD writing software is capable of converting the file to a pure VCD file as it is written to the CD.

MPEG-2 file is used on DVDs, satellite television, digital cable television, and HDTV. MPEG-2 yields highly compressed files of extremely high quality. MPEG-2 files and digital video files are of the same video resolution. NTSC MPEG-2 (DVD) is 704 by 480 pixels, while PAL MPEG-2 (DVD) is 704 by 576 pixels. This large resolution implies that the MPEG-2 file size is bigger than MPEG-1's. A two-hour movie will use up about four gigabytes of hard drive space. The most significant downside of MPEG-2 in terms of use on the Internet is system resources: MPEG-2 requires at least a 350-450 MHz CPU for reliable decoding and playback.

USB Instant DVD is an external device that connects to a USB port and enables the user to capture video directly from a camcorder, VCR, DVD player, DirectTV, Tivo or Replay PVR, or laser disk player in the proper MPEG-2 compression format. A USB Instant DVD allows the user to perform frame-accurate editing and create a final movie in DVD format.

DivX is a compression technology that facilitates large video transfer on high-speed modems. Using a model very similar to MPEG-4, full-screen movies are delivered at an amazingly small file size; DivX is popular for compressing and distributing DVD full-length videos and "theatre screen" dimension movies. Newer versions of DivX are often not compatible with the older versions.

H.263 video coding is often used in exporting e-mail and Web prefab settings. It is targeted toward smaller file size rather than superior quality. The H.263 standard, published by the International Telecommunications Union (ITU), supports video compression (coding) used for video-conferencing and video-telephony applications.

DV-PAL and *DV-NTSC* compression are used in very high-quality movies primarily for transferring video clips from camcorder to computer in the 16:9 widescreen format. By selecting the appropriate DV-PAL or DV-NTSC setting, all the imported clips will use the same specified pixel aspect ratio. Those using a standard video display monitor should select the 4:3 aspect ratio.

SVCD (Super Video CD) compression is used for DVDs and CDs. SVCD is actually MPEG-2 video but recorded at a lower bit rate and resolution than full broadcast resolution DVD. It provides an option of compressing a movie small enough to be played back on a CD configured for DVD playback or it can be configured for full DVD playback.

Compression Options

For Web usage, the playback performance is affected more by the pixel rate (how many pixels are drawn to the screen in a given second), rather than the data rate. If Web viewer delays are not an issue, the video producers can usually double the data rates. However, increasing the frame size and frames per second may influence playback performance and should be tested before making a final selection.

When preparing video for the Web, the video producers can use different frame rates to save bandwidth. They are not limited to 29.97 frames per second, which is necessary for television. When preparing videos for the Internet, developers can use a variety of compression tools on the video, but later go back to the original film. However, it is strongly advised to keep both horizontal and vertical dimensions a multiple of four (e.g. 240 wide is good; 241 is not).

Understanding the underlying principles of the compression settings will help the video producer achieve the quality of video desired. The following settings are available on most compression software:

- Quality Slider: Most compression formats provide a slider controlling general video quality, measured in percentage. Higher numbers result in larger file size and better quality. Default quality for most video compression is 50 percent.

- Data Type: Specifies video color bit depth, which determines the number of colors used. Normal video is 24-bit or 16 million colors. By reducing bit depth to 8-bit or 256 colors, the file size decreases, but areas of complex color will appear smudged and blurred. Reduced bit depth is largely drawings or cartoons or contains large areas of flat color. Not all compression types allow the user to reduce color bit depth.

- Data Rate: Data rate is the amount of video information that is processed during each second of playback. Some compression schemes let the user specify an ideal data rate for a particular movie. CD-ROM drives often boast data rate transfers in the 6 MB per second range. However, the recommended setting data transfer rates for playback on newer CD-ROM drives often exceed 1 MB per second while older drives at 300 k per second even though they are capable of much more.

- Keyframe: Keyframes contain all of the information required to display the frame. All videos contain at least one keyframe, which is the first frame of the file. After the first key frame, the software will automatically select other keyframes every time there is a sizeable change in content of the image. The compression scheme calculates and displays all colors in the keyframe. In non-keyframe frames, only the colors that have changed dramatically since the previous keyframe are calculated. The remaining keyframes serve to improve the quality of the video, but they also increase file size. Generally, video producers should try using one keyframe for every 10 seconds of video.

When compressing a video, the video producer needs to consider these issues. What video codec should be used? What will be the size of the picture? What will be the frame rate? Will a separate audio codec be used? What file size will be used? How will quality versus quantity be balanced?

Shooting Compression-Friendly Video

Shooting compression-friendly video is more difficult than shooting video that will be transferred directly to a VCR. The slogan to follow is "Mr. Rogers good, MTV bad." Detail and motion use the most bits in compressed video. The more complex the image and the more it moves, the more difficult it is for a codec to reproduce that image. Classic, sedate video shooting and editing will compress easily, while jump cuts, wild motion graphics, and handheld shaky camera work are difficult to compress at lower data rates.

While shooting on-location the cameraperson must remain aware of what is happening in the background. Simple background elements help with compression and detail and motion should be avoided.

If text is to be used on the video, font selection needs to be made with care. The sharp edges and details of small text are difficult to compress, especially if the video will be reduced to a smaller resolution.

Rapid cutting of a video can cause problems. At each cut, the change in the video content requires a keyframe to account for the big change in the content. A cut every 10 seconds is usually insignificant, but MTV-style editing, with a cut every second or less, can cause that section of video to be reduced to incomprehensible mush after encoding.

A cross-fade is one of the most difficult kinds of content to compress. Most of the tricks codecs use, do not work with blended frames of two different images. In these situations, each frame winds up a keyframe. It is much more efficient to use hard cuts. Fades to and from black are only slightly easier to compress than a cross-fade and should be avoided if possible. Wipes and pushes work quite well technically but are not appropriate stylistically for many projects. A straight cut is often the best bet.

Tip

When capturing video choose a compression setting that produces a better quality clip than needed. Users can always choose a lower quality compression setting when exporting the movie, but they cannot select a higher one.

Audio Compression

When producing video, users must always consider how the audio will affect the final project. Using audio in a video file always increases the file size, sometimes dramatically, which makes selecting audio compression options an important factor in keeping file size to a minimum. Audio compressed at a 20:1 or 10:1 ratio will certainly sound inferior to audio compressed at a 2:1 ratio.

Audio compression reduces the difference between the quietest and loudest parts of a song or other audio. The audio compressor has a threshold. The sound above the threshold is compressed while the sound beneath the threshold will not be affected. How high or low the threshold levels are set determines how much of the dynamic range will be affected.

If the video being uploaded contains music, it is best to maintain the audio quality at 44 MHz, 12- or 16-bit stereo. If the video has spoken works in which clarity is an issue, the producer can drop the quality to 22 MHz, but no further. If the quality goes lower than 22 MHz, by the time the project is distributed, the video will start to lose sibilance (the clarity of high-frequency sounds, such as the letter "s"), and interviewees will sound thick-tongued. If the video has crowd voices and incidental "Great to be here!" exclamations from the background, the video can be safely compressed down to 16 MHz, but no further. Audio compressed at 11 MHz sounds muddy and is not worth keeping.

The audio compression ratio determines the relationship between input and output. For example, if the ratio is set at 6:1 for every 6 dB of input above the threshold the user will only get 1dB of output, a steep compressor setting. It is possible to achieve a lot with a threshold setting between 3:1 and 6:1. If the compressor's ratio gets steep enough, it functions as a *limiter*. A limiter says to the sound wave, "You're not going much higher."

PCM audio stands for pulse code modulation and refers to uncompressed digital audio. PCM audio consists of one channel mono or two channels of stereo sound. Changing from mono to stereo essentially doubles the amount of space needed to store the file's audio, so stereo should only be used if necessary. For improved voice quality, instead of switching to stereo, it might be wiser to raise the frequency to 16,000 Hz.

Dolby Surround Sound 5.1 (pronounced "five dot one" or "five point one") is a codec from Dolby Laboratories called "Dolby AC-3" or just AC-3 and is used on many commercial DVD titles and is seen on commercial DVD boxes as Dolby Digital. A 5.1 surround sound system contains six discrete channels. (A discrete channel is completely separate from its accompanying channels. A stereo signal contains two discrete channels.) Five of the channels are full bandwidth, 20 Hz to 20 kHz, and the sixth channel—the ".1"— is for the basement lows, from 5 to 125 Hz. The 5.1 channels are referred to as left, right, center left surround, right surround, and LFE (low frequency effect).

Digital Still Photo Compression

Still digital photos are often incorporated into a video clip during the editing process. Therefore, an understanding of still photo compression is helpful. An uncompressed bitmap or *TIFF* image can take up 10 or 20 MB while compressing that same file into *JPEG* format make only take 275 kb.

The most common graphics file formats on the Web are those with the extensions *.jpg* and *.gif*. The .jpg extension is short for "Joint Photographic Experts Group" while the .gif extension stands for "Graphics Interchange Format". Both formats can be viewed on both the MAC and PC platform.

Lossy versus Lossless Compression

Lossy compression codecs discard some data contained in the original file during compression. A compression codec may or may not be lossy depending on how their quality and data rate options are set. Lossless algorithms, by definition, might not be able to compress the file any smaller than it started. Lossy codecs generally let the user specify a target data rate, and discard enough information to hit that data rate target. Its compression algorithm offers much higher compression ratios than lossless algorithms.

Lossy compression is only suitable for use on audio or graphical data. The audio or graphics are reproduced, but at a lower overall quality than they had before they were compressed. In some cases, the difference between lossy and lossless compression is difficult to perceive since the ratio in lossy compression can usually be adjusted so the quality level can vary widely.

Lossless compression is commonly used to reduce the size of computer files for electronic transmission. In order for the files to be useable on a computer, the files that are extracted from a compressed data file must be identical to the original file (before it was compressed). Lossless compression is necessary because it makes perfect copies, but it does not yield high compression ratios. Thus, it does not save large amounts of disk storage space. ZIP, ARC, TAR, and SIT are some of the acronyms or formats of lossless compression commonly used on computers.

ZIP files are "archives" used for distributing and storing files. Usually the files "archived" in a ZIP format are compressed to save space. These files make it easy to group files and make transporting and copying these files faster. ZIP files can be decompressed on the PC with *WinZip*.

Files can also be compressed using a program called *Stuffit Expander* for Mac or Windows, which makes a file with a .SIT extension. Both .SIT and .ZIP provide approximately a 2:1 compression.

With the increase in inexpensive mass storage and the increases in connection speeds, we are gradually approaching a point in time when digital compression may not be as important of an issue as it was in the past. The strength of lossless compressors specifically for digital audio provide the best of both worlds, a reduction in the amount of file storage space as well as no degradation in the quality of the audio or video data.

Summary:

While digital compression is one of the most difficult aspects of video editing, it is also one of the most important. Consideration of the compression of the final product should be considered from the pre-production phases, through the shooting of each scene, to the selection of transitions and special effects. The underlying question is, "How much quality should be sacrificed for optimum file size?"

Chapter

Videotaping and Capturing

Guidelines

In video production, an understanding of camcorders, microphones, and editing software is fundamental. However, those who never get beyond a basic understanding of video tools will only be considered good technicians. It is only after educators and students master the basic tools of video editing and are able to use those tools to express their ideas in creative and even artistic ways that their work can be considered praiseworthy and exemplary. The major role for production tools is to enhance, amplify, or explain the message.

Preparing a Videotape for Recording

Even the best shooting can be degraded by lack of care of the videotape. Certain precautions will prevent needless frustrations later. Before recording or storing a videotape, rewind it from end to end, in one complete, uninterrupted procedure to make sure the tape is wound evenly and uniformly. The official term for this process is "retensioning".

Never record from the very beginning of a videotape. When the camcorder begins recording, the actual tape is pulled outside its cassette case, wrapped around, and moves over a high-speed, rotating circular drum that contains two or four-moving recording heads. If the record stop control is hit, then the tape stops moving and is pulled back into its cassette case. The tape can never return to the exact location, causing a three or four second delay between pushing the record icon to start or stop a recording and the camera actually completing that process. Therefore, before pressing the record button, confirm that the videotape is cued to the proper position on the tape and that nothing of importance will be erased during the recording. Ideally, the recording should begin approximately 10 seconds past the end of the last recorded program.

Once the program ends, continue to record at least 10 seconds of black video and silence before stopping the tape! Extra footage serves to separate each program with a bit of black and prevents the ends of programs from being erased inadvertently by the following recording.

Preparing for an On-Location Scene

If a scene is to be shot on-location, it is vital to survey the site before the shoot. Look around and see where the scene will be shot. Make sure the background of the shot will not draw the viewer's attention from the main subject. Everyone has seen live television interviews shot on-location where somebody in the background is waving or making faces at the camera. Background clutter or distracting objects, like an overflowing garbage bin, can usually be avoided by repositioning the camera (moving it left or right, framing a tighter shot, changing the camera angle) or moving the subject.

In selecting a location, consider the following questions: Is there enough room for the camera crew and subject? When shooting, what will be behind the subject? Will AC power be used or will the camera run on batteries during the shoot? Will tungsten light be mixing with sunlight? Will the video be shot in front of a window or with the sun to the subject's back? Are there any unwanted noises occurring such as light hum, equipment buzz, children playing, cars going by, or planes flying over? Who is in charge of letting the video crew into the location to shoot and how can that person be contacted?

Shooting Tips

- The first frames shot should tell the audience where they are. The "establishing shots" are wide-angle shots of a sign, natural monument, historical reference, or any indication showing where the video is taking place. A shot of the Eiffel Tower says to the audience, "We're not in Iowa anymore."

- Before pressing the record button, shoot the video with editing rules in mind. Think about the final production before and during the shoot. By shooting to edit, the videographer will be able to edit faster and the results will be of much higher quality.

- During the actual shoot, keep the tape rolling whenever possible. It is easier to cut out lots of bad footage than to miss any good footage, especially when the subject is children, pets, or wildlife. One never knows when something special will happen.

- When shooting video, get plenty of A-roll (the main event) and B-roll footage (other shots). If it were a school soccer game, the videographer might get the action (the A-roll footage) and get some B-roll shots of the cheerleaders, the crowd, the coaching staff, and the team before and after the game.

- Learn to use the camcorder's manual controls. The auto focus on the camera can be fooled and search in and out. By using the manual focus, clearer pictures can be achieved.

- Use a light indoors. Even a low camcorder light will give colors that are more brilliant and there will be less generation loss while the video is edited, if there is adequate light.

- DO NOT overuse the zoom. A video that is constantly zooming in and out is difficult to watch.

- DO NOT pan back and forth. Pan in only one direction for each scene and avoid over-panning. (Pan right—The camera swivels to the right causing the image to move from right to left across the screen. Pan left—The camera swivels to the left causing the image to move from left to right across the screen.)

- DO NOT center the subject. Think of the television screen as a tic-tac-toe board and place important objects in the lines of the board, not in the middle. The video will look much better.

- Follow the action. The subject is moving yet stays within the frame because the camera is MOVING with the subject.

- Record 10 seconds of tape before the action starts and ten seconds after the action ends so there is room for fades or dissolve before or after the clip.

- Use insert shots and cutaways for added effect. The use of an insert shot is simply a way of directing attention to a significant element within the scene. The insert shot forces the audience to look at a significant aspect of the overall scene while highlighting details that may not have been apparent.

Composition

Composition consists of all the elements included in a scene. Even though the principles of good composition seem clear, they should be considered guidelines and not rules. Composition is an art, not a science. Since composition is an art, the guidelines can occasionally be broken. However, when composition guidelines are broken, it should be by someone who understands the principles and recognizes how a greater impact can be successfully obtained in a specific situation by breaking the rules. Unfortunately, the vast majority of individuals break the guidelines, because they are not "visually savvy", resulting in weak, confusing, and amateurish-looking work.

The first guideline in good composition is that content takes precedence over form. In other words, the intended message of a production is more important than technical excellence or flashy embellishments. Many students fall into this trap and spend more time on the flashy embellishment and little on intellectual content. Lack of content can be avoided by preparing a well-developed storyboard before beginning to shoot the video. In addition, significant technical problems—poor sound, a jittery camera, or a lens going in and out of focus—will quickly divert attention away from *the message*—content.

Secondly, a videographer should strive for a feeling of unity. A shot is said to have *unity* when the elements of the shot combine to support a basic visual statement. The concept of unity applies to such things as lighting, color, wardrobes, sets, and settings. The viewer must be able to recognize a relationship among all the elements within the frame.

The third guideline of composition applies to individual scenes. Each scene needs to be composed around a single center of interest. Multiple centers of interest may work in three-ring circuses where viewers are able to shift their interest from one event to another, but competing centers of interest within a single visual frame weaken, divide, and confuse the meaning. When shooting a scene with two people talking, make sure to give the room as they look at each other. Sometimes an over the shoulder shot is good to use in conversations. Each shot should be thought of as a separate statement.

The fourth guideline is to observe proper subject placement. Generally when a subject is moving in a particular direction, space is provided at the side of the frame for the subject(s) to "move into". Care should be taken to provide a pleasing amount of headroom, the amount of space between the top of a person's head and the top of the frame. Too much headroom makes the person appear to be sinking. Too little headroom places visual emphasis on the person's chin and neck. When framing shots of people, pay attention to where the eyes appear.

The *rule of thirds* should be considered before planning a shot. In the rule of thirds, the total image area is divided vertically and horizontally into three equal sections. Except possibly for people looking directly at the camera, it is often best to place the center of interest near one of the points indicated by the rule of thirds. A few still cameras even have the rule of thirds gridlines visible in their viewfinders. With the horizontal lines, put the subject either on top or below the middle.

Figure 8.1: Rule of Thirds

The most significant part of the picture should be where the lines intersect. There are four choices—top-left, top-right, bottom-left, bottom-right. When working with the horizon if a person wants to put the emphasis on the sky, then the horizon should be on the bottom third and if an emphasis on the ground is desired, the horizon should be on the top third.

The fifth composition guideline is to balance mass. Just as a room would seem out of balance if all of the furniture were stacked on one side, a scene must be balanced to be aesthetically pleasing. Regardless of their actual physical weight, large objects in a scene seem heavier than small ones. By objectively viewing the elements in a scene, the videographer can estimate their visual weight and rearrange the setting.

The sixth guideline is to maintain tonal balance. The tone (brightness and darkness) of objects in a scene influences visual weight. For example, against a medium background dark objects seem heavier than light objects. Once the videographer realizes how brightness influences mass, she can begin to "feel" the visual weight of objects within a scene and strive for balance.

The seventh composition guideline for visual composition is the pleasing use of lines. The boundaries of objects in a shot normally consist of straight, curved, vertical, horizontal, or diagonal lines. Our eyes tend to travel along these lines as they move from one part of the frame to another. The videographer needs to use these lines to lead the attention of viewers to the parts of the frame they wish to emphasize.

Another guideline is to use colors and tones to convey meaning. A scene that is dark with many large shadow areas (a dark bedroom or a back alley at midnight) produces a far different feeling from a scene that is brightly lit. The predominance of bright or dark areas carries strong psychological meaning in itself, regardless of what else is happening in the frame. In general, bright colors add energy to composition, while lighter hues impart a serene, harmonious, and stable look. When shooting a video, the videographer needs to keep the intended audience in mind since color preferences vary with age, sex, and race.

The last composition guideline maintains that the movement within the frames evokes meaning. Motion is generally from less significant to the more significant. For example, movement from dark areas to light areas can symbolize liberation or emotional uplift.

Upward motion, even something as simple as an individual rising from a chair, catches attention because it suggests progress or advancement. Downward movement suggests the opposite; for example, a woman collapsing into an overstuffed sofa suggests fatigue or emotional exhaustion. Action that moves toward the camera is more powerful than action moving away from the camera. Left-to-right movement is generally more engaging than right-to-left movement.

Field of View

Field of view camera shots are defined by how much of the scene is seen within the frame of the viewfinder. Changing the field of view can be controlled two different ways. One would be to change the distance between the camera and the subject by physically moving the camera closer or farther away. The other is to change the focal length of the lens, which controls the angle of view. A zoom lens is a combination wide angle, normal, and telephoto lens. The user can change the angle of view by zooming in to a narrow angle of view (telephoto) or zooming out to a wide angle of view.

Five basic shots make up the field of view in picture composition. The *long shot* (LS) frames a wide field of view of the subject and its surroundings. It usually requires a greater distance between the camera and the subject. Most likely the videographer would choose a wide-angle lens setting (zoomed out). Long shots are also referred to as wide shots or establishing shots, which establish the subject's location for the viewers by revealing its surrounding. This type of shot might be used to cover broad action involving several people in a large area. Long shots should be used sparingly because details are lost in long shots.

A *medium shot* (MS) frames more of the subject while still revealing some of the background. If the subject were a person, a medium shot would show the person from about the waist up. A medium close-up communicates gestures, broad expressions, and actions frames within close limits. Medium/Mid-range shots are use to communicate actions and interactions of characters.

A *close-up shot* (CU) focuses the viewer's attention on specific details. It demands that the viewer concentrate on the information being given them. In storytelling, close-ups have great emotional impact. Close-ups can also be used to give the audience information the characters in the video do not have. For example, showing a close-up of a sign reading "wet paint" right before a medium shot of the character in the process of sitting down on a painted park bench would build anticipation and set up the audience for the laugh. A close-up of a person would frame the subject from the top of the head to the top of the shoulders. Human emotions are best revealed in close-ups.

An extreme close-up shot (XCU) frames only a portion of the subject. It is a very dramatic shot that can generate great visual excitement. Extreme close-up shots are used to focus attention. Extreme close-up shots might be used to show the face of a wristwatch or words being typed on a computer screen. Like the long shot, extreme close-up shots should be used sparingly and only when it is critical to the meaning of the shot.

Figure 8.2: Field of View

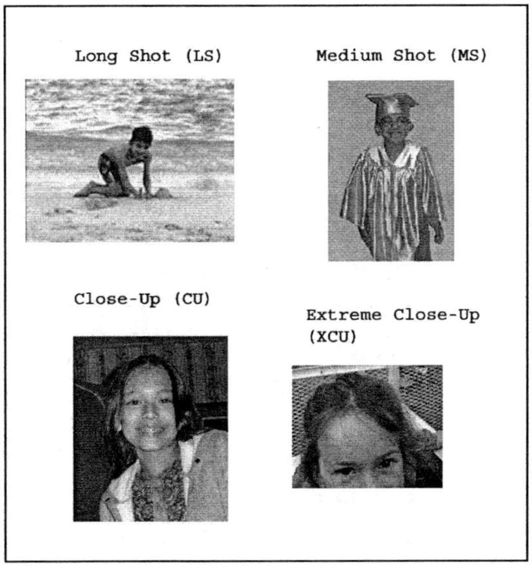

Long Shot (LS)

Medium Shot (MS)

Close-Up (CU)

Extreme Close-Up (XCU)

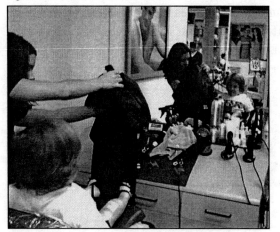

Figure 8:3: Point of View Shots

For best results, the videographer will want to move the camera physically as opposed to using the zoom features.

Point-of-View Shots

People interpret events differently based on how they see them. The cameraperson and the director can control an audience's sense of involvement in the story by controlling the position of the camera. An "objective camera" can be placed in a detached position where it records the action only as an observer while a "subjective camera" makes the audience feel a part of the action.

The *point-of-view shot* (POV) generally begins by shooting a person doing something or looking somewhere and then shoots from the subject's position, so the viewer can see what the subject was seeing. Being able to see what the viewer sees can be accomplished by having the subject move away or taping an over-the-shoulder shot. An over-the-shoulder shot draws the audience into the action, as if they are in the shot with the character.

Principles of Light

Figure 8.4: Worklights

Brightly lit rooms often deliver enough ambient light for videotaping. If available light will not provide most of the illumination, movie lighting should be added sparingly until the desired image is obtained. Adding reflectors is the obvious first step. When adding lights, first add fill lights that focus the light and heat away from the subject. If it is necessary to aim lights directly at subjects, keep them as far away as practical. The farther to the side they are, the less they shine in the talent's eyes. The danger in using natural light or a single key light with reflector fill is that the background can be neglected so that the subjects appear in a muddy limbo.

Other lights that can be added include an ultra-compact, focusable 1,000-watt halogen spotlight with four-way barn doors or a stand with a pair of 500-watt halogen lights. Portable clip-on lights with 250 or 300 watts from a local hardware store can be an inexpensive addition to add variety to the lighting choices of a video maker. These lights can be clipped on a stand or held by other students.

Big windows may provide nearly all the light a particular scene needs if they are to the side of the subjects. If direct sunlight streams through the window, use it as a key light. For a fill light, bounce the sunlight back from off-camera using reflectors on the opposite side.

If the background light is minimal, use the camera's backlight feature. The backlight feature allows the camera to compensate for overly bright light, but it does not add in background light as some people may think.

In one-point key lighting, the key light, or main light, is placed in front of the subject at a 45-degree angle and aimed down at the subject at a 45-degree angle. The key light establishes the dimension, form, and surface detail of subject matter. Attention to this light is extremely important when videotaping someone's face because subtle nuances of light can flatter or distort a facial feature. Although the remaining lights have less important roles, they are nevertheless critical in creating an acceptable lighting effect.

In two-point lighting the fill light and the key light work together. The purpose of the fill light is to soften the harsh shadows from the key light. The fill light is placed closer to the subject than the key light and about 90 degrees away from the key light. A person should be able to make a right angle by drawing lines from the key to the subject and then to the fill light. Since the fill light is less powerful than the key light, it should not be pointed directly at the subject. The fill light should be a floodlight, not a spotlight.

In three-point lighting, place the backlight above and in the back of the subject at a 60- to 70-degree angle of elevation. The back light separates the subject from the background, adds highlights to the subject's hair, and creates a three-dimensional effect. The back light should be a spotlight, not a floodlight. The function of the back light is to separate the subject from the background by creating a subtle rim of light around the subject. From an overhead perspective, a person should be able to draw a straight line from the lens of the camera through the subject, directly to the back light. By using only backlights with no front lighting, a silhouette effect will be created, which causes dramatic effects or hides someone's identity.

Background lights are used to illuminate the background area and add depth and separation between scene elements. (Remember that a back light is designed to light up the back of subjects and a background light is designed to light up the front of backgrounds.) Any type of light can be used as a background light as long as it provides fairly even illumination across the background, does not hit the central subject matter, and is at the appropriate intensity.

Color Basics

Every kind of light emits a certain color, and this is called the color temperature. Color temperature is measured using the *Kelvin scale, or K*. The higher the color temperature, the more bluish things are, the lower the color temperature, the more orange. Knowing the color temperature is important, as it makes it easier to adjust the manual white balance correctly.

If the camcorder has different settings for shooting video indoors or outdoors, it is often a good idea to use them. Florescent lighting is the one area where users will most likely have problems with white balance because florescent lights do not have the type of balanced mix colors that incandescent light and daylight have.

White Balance

Not all so-called white light is created equal. Within the range of what is typically considered normal white light, there are various shades, and objects videotaped under different lighting conditions appear differently.

White balance is the process by which the camcorder figures out what white looks like in a particular lighting situation and adjusts the color balance accordingly. Most camcorders today feature automatic white balance, which works well in most situations. Many camcorders allow users to manually set the white balance. Although the feature is accessed differently on different camcorders, the basic process is always the same:

1. Turn off the camcorder's automatic white balance feature.

2. Point the camcorder at a pure white subject. The subject should have a matte finish (not

glossy) and should take up 80 percent or more of the frame. A piece of white paper or a white T-shirt works great.

3. Focus the lens.

4. Push the white balance button or access the white balance menu to set the white balance.

After a videographer finishes shooting in a location using manual white balance, he needs to make sure to either turn automatic white balance back on, or adjust the white balance again at the new location. Turning off the camcorder and turning it back on will reset the white balance.

Using Filters and Gels

Lights tinted with color gels can correct white balance problems, create accents, and simulate off-screen lights. Digital color filters let the videographer do amazing things, but they can look digital. There is still no substitute for soft, natural-looking, colored light in video production. Glass filters drop right into the barn door rings of spotlights.

Some digital camcorders provide a *neutral density filter* (ND). ND helps in very bright situations where the camcorder's aperture, the opening in the camera lens, is at its very smallest. In these cases, the camcorder may have trouble providing a sharp focus. By applying the ND filter, the user is providing relief to the aperture control, which in turn increases the camera's ability to focus.

Makeup and Clothing

How the talent dresses for a video can have a tremendous impact on how effectively their message is received. Therefore, the talent should dress according to their part in the production. Having actors dress in the period attire and style adds authenticity to any performance. Realistic costuming can help the actor feel less self-conscious, allowing the character in the attire to emerge.

Some colors and patterns work better on video than others. For example, avoid small patterns and pinstripes, as they shift and move unnaturally on video. Horizontal striped clothing makes people look broader and shorter; vertical stripes make people look thinner and taller.

Solid colors are generally best, but bright white clothing under strong lights can sometimes glow and give a halo effect. Avoid overly bright, highly saturated colors like reds, oranges, and yellows, but use earth tones, especially browns, greens, and blues or pastel colors instead.

Television and video tend to add extra pounds on a performer and baggy clothing tends to compound that problem. Therefore, clothing should be simple and work well with the setting and theme of the video.

While listening to someone, either on a video, television, or in person, the attention is naturally directed to the speaker's face. As the center of attention, the talent's face requires careful makeup. There are three basic reasons to use facial makeup: to improve appearance, to correct appearance, and to change appearance.

Makeup allows the talent's skin tones to appear natural on the video. To achieve a natural look, begin with a foundation that evens out skin tone and serves as the base for the makeup to follow. Choose the shade of the foundation carefully, matching the natural skin tone of the talent as closely as possible. A general rule of thumb is that warm colors are best for video and television since the lighting already accentuates the cool colors.

There is a difference in makeup techniques from the stage to those for video. Stage makeup dramatically highlights facial features, so the audience can see them from the last row in the theater. For video, it is necessary that everyone look good in close-up. The bright lights tend to wash people out making them corpse-like. Properly applied makeup brings them back to life.

Hair plays a significant role in the on-camera appearance of talent. Both the style of the hair and overall grooming must complement the performers "look". Usually the best strategy is to choose one hairstyle and stick with it. It is important that the talent maintain the same hairstyle throughout the shoot because several unexplained changes in appearance can be confusing to the viewer.

Summary:

The major role for production tools is to enhance, amplify, or explain the message. The intended message of a production is more important than technical excellence or flashy embellishments. Many of the basic composition guidelines used in still photography also apply to video production as well. A good video clip must portray unity, balance, and pleasing lines. Lighting and color is extremely important in developing the mood of the action while the dress and makeup of the talent must be consistent with the intended message.

Chapter 9

Audio Production Tips

S ound is often considered more important than pictures. The mind can watch jumpy, jarring, and disjointed images, and if the sound is smooth and continuous, the brain will adjust. However, the opposite is not true; noises, blips, and jarring audio cuts will ruin an otherwise decent stream of video. Therefore, as much care, if not more, should be given to the audio portion of a video as is given to the visual effects. Digital audio technology is more fascinating than its analog predecessor, but it is built on many of the same principles.

Sound has two basic characteristics that must be controlled—volume and frequency, which is the specific pitch of the sound. Sound for a digital multimedia project can be downloaded from the Internet, recorded directly from the video source, or recorded separately and used as a voice-over.

Volume

Sound is a vibration that travels in waves through almost any medium, including air and water. Sound cannot travel in a vacuum. Sound is measured by its pitch, loudness, and speed. The loudness of a sound (called volume) is measured in decibels. Volume depends on how many air molecules are vibrating and how strongly they are vibrating. The quietest sound that can be heard has a value of zero decibels, the louder the sound, the higher the decibel level. For acoustics, 0 dB often means the threshold of hearing. Examples of sound-pressure decibel levels are given here in Figure 9.1.

Audio recording and editing devices contain meters that monitor incoming sound levels, and a volume control to adjust those levels. Whether a person records and edits to a hard drive, tape, or mini-disc, the fundamentals are the same.

Figure 9.1: Decibel Chart

Sound	Decibels
Silent TV Studio	20
Whisper at 10 Feet	30
Office Environment	45
Quiet Conversation/Phone Dial Tone	60-80
Restaurant/Average City Street	70-75
Subway/Jackhammer at 50 Feet	85-90
Rock concerts/Gunshots	135-140
Jet Aircraft Taking Off	140-150

Figure 9.2: Volume Meter

The volume meters should register within reasonable levels: high enough (just into the red) to mask the noise (inherent in all recorders) but not too high (always in the red) as to make the recorder distort. Digital recorders (digital audio tape, mini-disc, or computer) are much less noisy and more sensitive to distortion than analog (cassette or reel).

The 0 dB point on the volume meter is just a reference point. Therefore, it is possible to have a sound level on the meter that registers in negative dBs, just as it is possible to have a temperature of -10 degrees Centigrade or Fahrenheit.

The dB level going through audio equipment can be controlled carefully. If the signal is allowed to pass through equipment at too low a level, noise can be introduced when the level is later increased to a normal amplitude (audio level). If the volume level is too high, (significantly above 0 dB or into the red areas on the VU meter) distortion will result, especially with digital audio.

Frequency

Frequency relates to the basic pitch of a sound, how high or low the sound is. A frequency of 20 Hz would sound like an extremely low-pitched note on a pipe organ—almost a rumble. At the other end of the scale, 20,000 Hz would be the highest pitched sound that most people can perceive, even higher than the highest note on a violin or piccolo.

Frequency is measured in Hertz (Hz) or cycles per second (CPS). A person with exceptionally good hearing will be able to hear sounds from 20 to 20,000 Hz. Since both ends of the 20 to 20,000 Hz range represent extreme limits, the more common range used for television or video production is from 50 to 15,000 Hz.

The Frequency-Loudness Relationship

Even though sounds of different frequencies may technically be equal in loudness (register the same on a VU meter), human hearing may not perceive them as being of equal strength. Because of the reduced sensitivity of the ear to both high and low frequencies, certain sounds must be louder to be perceived as being equal to other frequencies.

Equalizers

Equipment and listening conditions greatly affect how different frequencies will be perceived. To compensate for some of these problems, users can adjust bass and treble controls of playback equipment. Sophisticated audio equipment includes a graphic equalizer, which allows specific bands of frequencies to be adjusted for loudness individually.

A graphic equalizer may be necessary to match audio segments recorded under different conditions, or simply to customize audio playback to the acoustics of a specific listening area. The reason television commercials are often louder than the program is that they were recorded under different conditions, and the sounds have not been controlled through an equalizer correctly.

Any equalization used during the course of production should remain consistent throughout the audio tracks. Although it may be tempting, the novice user should avoid attempting to improve location soundtracks by means of equalization. Adjusting the highs, mid-range, and bass from shot to shot may sound fine in the headphones, but when shots are cut during the editing process, changes in voice and backgrounds often become annoyingly apparent.

Room Acoustics

Sound, both as it is recorded and played back, is affected more by the acoustics of a room or studio than most people realize. In an effort to create totally soundproof studios, early radio stations used thick carpets on the floors and heavy soundproofing on the walls. Although possibly successful as soundproofing, the result was a lifeless and dead effect that we are not used to hearing in a normal environment. At the other extreme from a room with carpeted walls, is a room with a tile floor and hard, parallel walls that reflect sound. The result is reverberation (a slight echo) that interferes with the intelligibility of speech.

The ideal room for recording or listening to sound has just enough reverberation to sound realistic, similar to a living room, but not enough to reduce the intelligibility of speech. The ideal sound environment is usually achieved only by trial and error to discover what works best in a given situation.

Sources for Digital Audio to Include in Video

Audio from a DV Camera

Digital audio from a digital video camera DAT (*digital audio tape)*, is a high-quality sound (48 kHz) most often used with video clips. One drawback of using this source is that the camera's built-in microphone is of marginal quality. For more professional sounding shoots, high-quality external microphones need to be used in conjunction with a mixer.

Music CDs

Music CDs are high quality at 44 kHz. The music may be protected by copyright, so student video makers must first check the Fair Use Laws or obtain official permission before using commercial CDs.

Microphones

Video makers can record their voice directly into the computer with a microphone. Before using a computer microphone, the user needs to first open the sound control panel to make sure the volume is on and up, and that the 'Sound In' is set to microphone.

Downloadable MIDI Files

MIDI is the acronym for Musical Instrument Digital Interface. MIDI is a digital language agreed upon by major manufacturers of electronic musical instruments. It allows keyboards, synthesizers, computers, tape decks, and even mixers and stage light controllers to talk to each other. MIDI files do not contain actual audio. Instead, the music sequence is recorded as a series of numbers, which explain how the music is to be played back. The advantage of a MIDI file is that it is very small. The sound is completely dependent on the output device (usually the sound card in the computer) and can be easily edited.

Since MIDI files are only text instructions written to a synthesizer, and would not be able to work in a video as is, *QuickTime Pro* and other such programs can convert the MIDI files into AIFF files. Because MIDI files only describe notes (pitch, volume, duration and instrument), they are good only for instrumental music, not for vocals. The Internet is full of free, downloadable MIDI files because anyone with a computer and a MIDI keyboard can create a file and upload it. One source of free MIDI files is <http://www.aitech.ac.jp/~ckelly/ SMF.html>, which is searchable by song titles linked to one or more downloadable versions of the song.

The downloaded songs will come in as a QuickTime MIDI file and should play in the middle of the screen. To save the song to a project folder, click on the down arrow in the lower-right-hand corner of the QuickTime Player Pro window. To convert the MIDI file to an aiff file that can be used in a video, with the file open click on FILE and then EXPORT. In the Export pop-up menu, choose MUSIC to AIFF or WAVE then save the file to the project folder.

Downloadable MP3 Files

An *MP3* file is an audio file that has been compressed so that it can be sent easily over the Net. MP3s are typically 1/10th the uncompressed size, with only a slight loss in quality. Most MP3 files are copyrighted music. These files cannot be used without permission or meeting Fair Use Guidelines.

To incorporate an MP3 file into a video, simply download the MP3 song to the project folder. Open QuickTime Player Pro and then open the MP3 file, click on FILE and then EXPORT. In the Export pop-up menu, choose MUSIC to AIFF or WAVE and then save it to the project folder.

Ripping is a term used when .wav files on a music CD are converted to MP3 files that can be stored and played on a computer or other digital media player. The downside of ripping from MP3 to WAV is that .wav file sizes are large; a full 74 minute audio CD uses approximately 650 MB storage space. Musicmatch JukeBox, RealOne Player, and Sonic Foundry Siren have free CD-ripping and MP3 creation options.

Audio Channels

The more audio channels used, the greater the file size. Twice the channels equal twice the file size. As users weigh their options and available file space, they must assess the importance of quality sound in the video versus storage capacity. If the piece stands on its own without simple sound, a single, monophonic channel would be sufficient.

If sound is important, then another discrete channel can be added. In stereophonic, two complementary channels lead to two loudspeakers, which provide a more natural depth to the sound than a single mono channel.

Currently, Dolby Surround Sound with six discrete audio channels has the highest quality of sound. Five of the channels are full bandwidth, 20 Hz to 20 kHz, and the sixth channel—the ".1"—is for the basement lows, from five to 125 Hz, although the idea of a speaker's subwoofer reproducing down to 5 Hz is theoretical. Dolby Surround Sound is becoming extremely popular on DVDs and is included on many DVD-burning programs.

Selecting the Right Microphone

Microphone elements: elements are the part of a microphone that gather sound and convert it into electrical audio signals that can be processed by audio mixers and camcorder. There are two types of elements used in microphones used by schools: the dynamic element and the condenser element. Each element has particular characteristics that make it useful in specific situations.

Dynamic microphones once were the basic workhorses of the film and video industries although, in recent years, there has been a changeover to *condenser microphones*. However, dynamic microphones still remain important tools for the production sound mixer. They can be counted on to work when other microphones may not. Dynamics do not require batteries or powering of any sort and are extremely rugged.

Dynamics are recommended for recording location narration, since they isolate voice from background sounds extremely well and are useful for recording loud and sudden sound effects, such as crashes and explosions. Not only are dynamic microphones resistant to damage from high noise levels, but they also tend to compress or dampen the audio in such a way to make these sounds easier for the recording electronics to handle.

Microphones with condenser elements are used for recording high-quality moderate-to-soft sounds such as voice, music, and special news reports. Using a condenser microphone requires care because the condenser element is more fragile than its dynamic counterpart. Unlike microphones that use the dynamic element, condenser microphones require a power source. That power source may be a battery installed in the microphone handle or in a separate battery pack. Some condenser microphones require phantom power, which is power that is provided by the audio mixer.

Microphone directionality: microphones differ in the direction they pick up sound. The *omni-directional* microphone picks up sounds from all directions in the environment. The *unidirectional* microphone, also known as cardioid, picks up sounds from the front or top of the microphone and very little from the sides or back in a heart shape pattern.

Some microphones have a stronger directional pattern and may be called super-, hyper-, or ultra-cardioid microphones. The highly directional microphones are used to record specific sources from a distance or block out unwanted sounds in a noisy setting. Directional microphones are far more sensitive to wind and pop noises than omni-directional microphones due to the use of more compliant diaphragms on directional microphones, which are more easily excited.

A majority of the production dialogue recorded in major "Hollywood" theatrical productions and television series use microphones from overhead, utilizing either a fishpole or studio boom. Overhead miking provides a natural sound with normal sound effects and some background ambiance.

Shotgun Microphones

The most popular microphones for exterior use are long shotgun microphones. The shotgun microphone was named because the long, slotted tube in front of the microphone cartridge makes it resemble a shotgun. Similar to telephoto lenses, shotgun microphones tend to compress the distance between foreground and background. This "interference tube" helps to reject sounds coming from more than about 30 degrees off to the sides, while still picking up sounds from the front. This directional pickup pattern (called a line/gradient pattern) makes shotgun microphones popular for television news and on movie sets.

While using a shotgun, the user should avoid pointing the microphone as if it were a rifle, unless background noise is not important. The best way to eliminate this "telephoto" audio effect is to aim the microphone down from above so that the only background in the microphone line of sight is the silent ground. The disadvantages of the long shotgun are its directionality and physical dimensions. The narrow pick-up pattern requires that more care be taken in aiming the microphone.

Surface Mounted Microphones

Surface mounted microphones are designed to work on a flat surface. They are usually contoured to look less intrusive on a conference table or desktop. The microphone element is located very close to (but not touching) the surface, which allows it to take advantage of the reflected sound as well as the direct sound.

Pressure Zone Microphone (PZM)

A *pressure zone microphone* (PZM) is a flat microphone that resembles a fly swatter without the handle. The PZM lies flat on any surface and becomes a conductor for the sound. It works well for recording group discussions or a hidden microphone for dramatic or fictional videos. Most PZMs are condenser microphones.

Wireless Microphones

A lavaliere microphone is defined as being any small microphone designed to be worn on a performer's body. Lavalieres are omni-directional so they pick up sound from all directions. The lavalieres are generally "proximity" oriented and work best when the sound source is close to them. This close-up sound emphasizes the voice and holds back the ambiance, which are both the strength and the weakness of the lavaliere microphone.

Lavaliere microphones leave the speaker's hands free to gesture, hold notes, or demonstrate a product. In addition, they are usually small and tend to "disappear" on camera. Using a lavaliere will help keep the distance from the microphone to the speaker's mouth constant, reducing the need for frequent mixer adjustments once levels have been set.

Some of the problems that may be encountered with lavalieres include the difficulties of hiding them under clothing, clothing noise, wind noise, and the loss of audio perspective in relation to the camera (the dialog always sounds "close-up" regardless of framing). For best results, lavalieres should be clipped to the tie or lapel at the breast pocket level.

Wireless microphones can be categorized as handheld, body pack, or plug-on; VHF or UHF; and diversity or non-diversity. Most professional units share the upper VHF television bands (TV channels seven through 13) and could have some interference with a local station.

Wireless microphones are available in the UHF frequency range. The UHF frequencies are less susceptible to most common sources of radio interference than VHF. More UHF units can be operational at the same time without cross interference and the transmitter antennas on the body packs are very short and do not require careful rigging to the actor's clothing.

The most common kind of microphone is the handheld type that has built-in transmitters. The handhelds are popular with vocalists and variety stage performances because the user can hold it, mount it on a floor or desk stand, or attach it to a flexible "gooseneck" on a lectern.

Tip

Whether held in the hand or mounted on a stand, the microphone should be positioned about six to 12 inches from the speaker's mouth, pointing up at about a 45-degree angle.

A good quality handheld microphone should have an internal shock mount, which will minimize handling noise (thumping sounds transmitted through the handle and picked up by the microphone cartridge), and it should be ruggedly constructed to withstand physical abuse.

Body packs consist of transmitters only and are more like a "wireless cable" rather than "wireless microphones", because any microphone (with the appropriate adapter cable) may be plugged into them. Body pack transmitters are generally used with lavaliere microphones. Wireless units can also be used with a condenser microphone on a fishpole or a stationary microphone planted on the set.

Body pack transmitters can be hidden almost anywhere. The most common sites include the small of the back, rear hip, inside thigh, ankle, pants pocket, and inside chest pocket of a jacket, or in the heroine's purse. When placing the transmitter and receiver, strive to maintain minimum distance between them. Move the receiver/antenna from shot to shot in order to achieve close and clean line-of-sight placement.

Virtually anything can interfere with good radio transmission and cause bursts of static. Check for metallic objects such as jewelry, zippers, coins, and keys. If the metal cannot be eliminated, then the antenna on the talent should be repositioned.

Foam Windscreens

Foam windscreens and pop filters are intended to provide protection against low velocity moving air, such as would be encountered from performers exhaling onto the microphone. Foam windscreens also protect sensitive condenser microphones against the motion of room air caused by normal ventilation ducts as well as from the physical act of moving the microphone while mounted on a boom pole. Although some handheld performance microphones come equipped with built-in wind or pop protection, condenser microphones should never be used without a protective windscreen.

Microphone Problems

Feedback is a condition when the microphone picks up the sound, amplifies it, radiates it to a speaker, and then picks it up again and re-amplifies it. Eventually the system starts to ring and keeps howling until the volume is reduced. Feedback occurs when the sound from the loudspeaker arrives at the microphone as loud as, or louder than, the sound arriving directly from the original sound source, whether it is a speaker or singer.

The right microphone will help reduce the problem of feedback. While a good omni-directional microphone might work well in some situations, a directional is usually preferred where a high potential for feedback exists. The directional microphone can be aimed to minimize pickup of the loudspeaker's sound that might be reflected from the walls, ceiling, or floors.

Distance is also a factor in the creation of feedback. Moving the microphone (or speaker) to lengthen the acoustic path to the loudspeaker can often reduce feedback. Bringing the microphone closer to the intended sound source will also help.

Distortion is a measure of signal impurity. It is usually expressed as a percentage or decibel ratio of the undesired components to the desired components of a signal. Distortion levels should be considered when choosing between directional and omni-directional microphones since directional microphones tend to distort more than omni-directional.

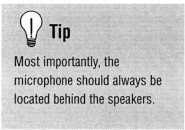

Tip

Most importantly, the microphone should always be located behind the speakers.

For detailed use of microphones, from placement tips to microphone construction technology, there are several online sites available. An excellent source is the Microphone University <http://www.dpamicrophones.com>. The sponsor of Microphone University is DPA Microphones, a leading manufacturer of high-quality condenser microphones and microphone solutions.

Recording Directly into a Computer

Even the most basic internal sound card has three connections: microphone in, line in, and line (or headphone) out. To record directly into a computer, connect the equipment by plugging the microphone into the mixer (or preamp) and plug the output of the audio mixer into the sound card's line in, then connect the headphones to the computer. Next, set the volume at the mixer (or preamp) using its controls and level meters. Start a test speech, watch the meters, and slowly raise the volume until you get close to 0 (zero) without going over.

Launch the software that controls the sound card; it is usually a little speaker icon in the system tray at the bottom of the screen. Select the recording source (line in) and adjust its volume. Set the volume at 100 percent—all the way up—since the external mixer or preamp will be controlling the recording level. Start the audio-recording software and find the record ready mode. Record a voice in mono, not stereo, and at CD quality, which is 16 bits, and 44 kHz sampling rate. Notice that the audio software does not have controls for setting levels, but the user can rely on its meters when recording and adjust the volume to his voice. Never exceed 0 (zero) on the digital level meters since anything above that level will become distorted.

To improve the sound quality of the recordings, get closer to the microphone. The farther the speaker is from microphone, the more ambient distortion is picked up from the room. Before recording, turn away from the microphone, take a deep breath, exhale, take another deep breath before opening your mouth, turn back to the microphone, and begin to speak. This technique eliminates the sharp intake of breath and lip smack that often occur when people start to speak.

Editing Audio Clips

Editing sound is much like editing in a word processor. A person will not see the words, but a two-dimensional representation of the words in sound waveforms. Words can be heard as they are played. These waveforms can be manipulated just as words in a word processor can be manipulated.

Besides cutting unwanted audio and varying the volume and frequency, audio editing software can be used to screen out some of the motor noise without affecting the rest of the sound on the tape. Many consumer video editors do not allow this and users may choose to use an audio-editing software such as *Cool Edit 2000*.

Summary:

In a video production, sound is often considered more important than the picture. Therefore, as much care needs to be given to audio editing as is given to video editing. For better quality video, students must move beyond depending solely on the built-in microphone of the camcorder, and learn to use the wide selection of consumer microphones on the market today. After students have captured the sound for the video, they will be amazed at the possibilities of changes that can be created digitally as they learn to edit the audio for their final production.

Chapter 10

Digital Video Editing

Recording a moving image is *capturing* time, while editing a moving image is *cheating* time. If a person wants the power to tell stories, create moods, and make time speed up, slow down, or insert a different version of time, the person must learn how to edit video. Many video-editing software programs with varying levels of sophistication are available, but the basic principles of digital video editing apply to all.

The first step in editing a video project is to gather all the anticipated video, images, and sound files into the same folder or program library. A video project contains two distinct kinds of files: media files, which are the actual video; and the project information, which is the small part that contains data about the video. Editing software stores these two types of files separately. The media files can be deleted while keeping the project files on the computer.

Media files come to two basic forms—picture and sound. A digital video camera records sound onto the tape at the same time it records the pictures and then plays them back synchronized. Most of the complexity of video editing comes from artfully managing the picture and sound tracks as well as adding other tracks, images, transitions, and special effects.

Many video-editing software programs ask the user to select format settings when the program first opens. Format setting choices can sometimes be confusing, but the rule of thumb is that larger video size, frame rate, and bit rate deliver better quality, but better quality will also result in much larger file sizes. If a user is customizing a video template, diligence needs to be taken in choosing the correct settings. The frame size to transfer to a video tape will need to be 640 by 480, but output back to a digital video camera will need to be 720 by 480 NTSC or 720 by 576 for PAL along with the audio sample rate of 48 kHz. If the wrong frame size or audio sample rate is selected, the camcorder may not be able to read the output.

Storyboard and Timeline View

Most video-editing software contains both a storyboard and a timeline view. In the storyboard view, a small thumbnail picture, known as the *keyframe*, represents the first image of each section of each video or image file. The user can simply drag videos and image files onto the storyboard where they can see the sequenced media at a glance.

The storyboard view is best used for dragging, dropping, and ordering clips, but it does not accurately reflect the length of each clip. Video clips generally cannot be shortened or lengthened in storyboard view, nor can media be "stacked" on top of one another. For these tasks, a timeline view is required, which allows the user to move around the sequence of clips, add additional video and audio tracks, and add effects and transitions.

Switching between storyboard and timeline view does not change the project, only the way it is viewed. A timeline view is essential for managing multiple tracks, while the storyboard mode is used to view all the project clips at a glance, noting sequence, and dragging clips to a new location in the project.

Cutting, Deleting, and Inserting Video Clips

Deleting segments from a clip used in a project does not alter the actual clip; it merely specifies which segments should be used in a particular project's storyboard. To add additional clips, a user needs only to drag the clip into the storyboard or timeline.

For close edits, zooming in on a few frames is essential for cutting and trimming precisely. Close edits are also critical on the audio track to make sure a song starts exactly when a particular on-screen event occurs.

To sequence clips in the timeline view, users merely drag the clips onto the timeline in the desired location. Clips can be removed from the timeline by dragging them out of the timeline back to the shelf. The order of the video clips can be changed by clicking, dragging, and dropping the clips into new locations on the timeline. If the user clicks on a clip in the clip view, the monitor will display the clip and allow further trimming and cropping.

Before trimming a video clip, the user needs to identify the IN and OUT points of the clip. The in point represents where the clip will begin playing, and the out point represents where it is to end. When a clip is cropped, the user trims the part of the clip to be kept. When a user cuts a clip, the in and out points to be eliminated in the clip are selected and that portion of the clip is deleted. In changing the in and out points, the program only changes the pointers in the video file to a new location on the footage and leaves the unwanted footage intact. Retaining the original clip allows for undoing overzealous trimming and restores the clip to its original state without having to recapture the footage.

To duplicate a clip, click once on the clip desired and then go to edit and to copy and then to paste. Duplicating a video clip is much the same copy-and-paste process used in a word processing program.

Transitions between Clips

Every video-editing package provides several options for transitioning from one clip to another. Each transition communicates a mood in its own way. Rather than bumping two clips side by side and getting a choppy project, a good video editor adds a transition that merges the end of the one clip with the beginning of another clip creating a smooth and continuous flow.

Video edits usually flow from track A to track B. These video transitions are sometimes referred to as "*A/B rolls*" because the contents of track A will roll into track B. The A shot is the outgoing shot, and its last frame is the outgoing frame while the B shot is the incoming shot.

A simple cut from one clip to the next is a neutral transition that does not communicate anything to the audience. A fade-in from black signifies an end. A cross dissolve, in which the first clip begins the fade-out while the next clip appears to fade in, is a smooth transition that signifies continuity.

Generally, each video shot relates to the shot before it and after it. When this order does not happen, a *jump cut* occurs. Jump cuts happen because of poor editing or lack of consistency while shooting or editing. To achieve a smooth-flowing video, care must be given to the impact and duration of each transition between video clips.

Adding Texts and Titles to Video

A title is wording added to a video using the titling tool in the video editor or a third-party editor. Titles are necessary in most videos to summarize briefly the important information. The value of titling a video is that the video creator has the ability to move words across the screen or have them easily appear and disappear. Used at the beginning, a title introduces something (an opening title) and at the end as "credits" that roll by. To apply text in the middle of a clip, the user must split the clip at the point at which the text is to begin. The clip may also have to be split if the text is to be applied at the beginning of a clip that already has a transition.

Guidelines for Preparing Titles

- Titles should be white text on a dark (or black) background.

- Titles are clearer if they are done in a *sans-serif font*. (There are two styles of fonts: serif and sans serif. This book is printed in a serif font. This is a sans-serif font. The difference is in the end strokes of each letter—"sans" is French for "without," as "without a curling end stroke.")

- Title font should be large enough to be read by anyone.

- Use semi-bold and boldface type weights.

- Make sure the titles remain on the screen long enough to be read.

- Keep the opening titles simple.

- If detailed text is needed, put it at the end, preferably over black keeping the audio running underneath.

- Fade the titles in and out.

- Select font colors with care. Red or other bright, saturated colors tend to bleed over the type and create a fuzzy look, so avoid them. Dark gray fonts will get lost on a black background.

- Titles should be distinguishable from the background and not compete with the background. If the background is busy, keep the titles a solid color. If the background moves, keep the type out of the line of movement.

Adding Still Images to Videos

When making a video, the audience can be lost by ineffective use of images and sound. Although some may think that constantly moving, quick-action video is the best way to keep the audience's attention, that is often not the case. Sometimes, the viewer needs to dwell on a picture or text to internalize the significance of a message.

To add a still picture into a video clip, a single video frame can be extracted and saved as a still picture. Every second of video is composed of 30 potential still images. In preparing still images for use within a video, the still should be changed to the aspect ratio 4:3 (640 by 480). Digital video records footage in 3:2 aspect ratio, but when it is played back on TV it conforms to the 4:3 aspect ratio of the TV. If the aspect ratio is not corrected in a still image, all digital video stills will look abnormally wide.

Pictures that have been prepared in a photo editing software package can be imported into the timeline. The prepared graphic should be placed in frames of correct proportion to fit on the screen. If not, there will be weird black bands on the top and bottom or left and right of the video when it is complete.

In video, it is common to refer to frame size as *resolution*. The term resolution has a slightly different meaning for video than it does for print media. Although the number of pixels in full-screen video can differ, a user can think of the display size as being fixed; it is full-screen, regardless of the size of the television screen. Therefore, it is best to think of digital video in terms of pixel dimensions, not pixels per inch. People who are accustomed to print media are often disappointed to learn that standard-definition video always translates to a mere 72 dpi.

Usually the default file format for still photos is Bitmap (BMP). Later a more efficient file format (like JPEG) can be used. The format chosen for an image file is a balancing act between compression practicality and personal preference and clarity. Avoiding the use of files with unnecessarily high resolutions not only saves disk space but also saves the editor program from needing as much memory. Lower resolution also will speed up the rendering process.

There are many ways still photos can be incorporated into a video. The obvious is to display a still instead of a video clip. Users now have options for displaying still photos that include the ability to pan and zoom over the image giving an impression of motion, use a picture-in-picture effect of a small still inserted into a video, create a moving montage of several stills, and many other movements that are limited only by the creator's imagination.

Inserting PowerPoint Slides into a Video

- The graphics and text in a *PowerPoint* slide nearly always run off the sides of the TV screen when used in a video. To correct this, export the slides using FILE/SAVE AS—select PNG, BMP, and JPEG.

- Scale each slide to the safe zone size ratio of 4:3.

- Adjust the colors and levels of the fonts and graphics used in the *PowerPoint* to avoid ringing, artifacting, or banding.

Special Effects

Most nonlinear-editing systems contain a generous special effects menu that includes slow motion, fast motion, strobe, and reverse image, and a multitude of other digital effects. Users can apply special effects to a portion of a clip, an entire clip, or a portion of the video that spans multiple clips. However, the overuse of special effects can distract the viewer or slow the computer.

To add an effect to a video clip, the computer must do many mathematical calculations for every pixel in every affected frame. Newer computers with fast CPUs can do this math more quickly than older ones. Using a slower computer means the video creator will have to wait while the computer renders the video. If the user does not like the effect seen and wants to change it, the computer will have to re-render, starting the whole process over again.

Video filters are special effects that can dramatically change the video's appearance. These filters for color correction, lens adjustments, lighting and shape effects, or alterations that are just plain strange to look at, can be applied to an entire video, a still image, or a short video segment that has been cut from a larger clip.

Masks and overlays blend one video with another video or image, allowing only a portion of the original to show through. To create an overlay, the user first determines which part of the video on the lower layer will be visible and which part will be hidden so the editing program can set up a mask to hide the unwanted portion.

Adding Multiple Audio Tracks— Voice Over, Music, Sound Effects

Picture and sound are two entirely different forms of media. The digital video camera records sound at the same time it records the pictures on the same tape and then plays them back synchronized. Most of the complexity of editing comes from managing the two tracks – pictures and sound.

Three categories of sound include dialog, music, and effects. *Voice overs* and narration are types of dialog tracks. Music establishes the mood and style of the final video. Music and narration have natural beats. The video needs to follow the sound, so the sound enhances the video.

Background music can have a greater impact on a video than the creator may intend. Before adding music to a video, the video creator needs to listen to the music first and feel the flow of the rhythm and the movement. Does the mood and rhythm of the music match the particular scene in question?

Adding Multiple Video Layers

Video compositing is a cross between animation and video editing. Video compositing enables the user to animate static images or video files across another static image backdrop or a moving video background. Using video compositing, the user can create the illusion of a person flying or levitating. The most popular video composition program is Adobe *After Effects* priced over $600 for the standard version and $1,200 for the professional version. *After Effects* has a steep learning curve. Lower level editing programs with basic 2D compositing controls include *VideoWave* and Adobe *Premiere* that allow the user to make objects float around the room with motion settings.

When creating video compositions involving several video layers, the lowest layer should be considered the canvas. The canvas can be a full-sized video, color frame, or still image while the other videos moving around the screen are not full-sized.

The transparency or opacity of a video clip can be increased or lowered in many editing programs. This feature is most effective in preparing ghost scenes or mysterious locations and moods.

Adding Chroma Key (Green/Blue Screen Effect)

The green/blue screen process is technically referred to as *Chroma Keying* (or just *keying*) because the creator selects a key color, which is then removed. Chroma Key technology controls the opacity of a video track that allows the user to layer video tracks on top of each other and see through the top video track into other video tracks below. Chroma Keying was once the exclusive domain of Hollywood special effects artists, but now, blue or green screen imaging has expanded to include school and home videos and computers.

Creating a green screen composite image starts with a subject being videotaped in front of an evenly lit, bright, pure green (or blue) background. The compositing process, done by the video-editing software, replaces all the green (or blue) in the picture with another image, known as the background plate. Green screen backgrounds can be made from still photos or movies, or live videos.

Background plates for Chroma Keying can easily be made or purchased for a classroom or media center. The standard paints used to create a Chroma Key background are from Rosco, the light gel manufacturer. Blue and green fabrics and drapes can also be purchased and hung behind the set. Backlit screens are also commercially available from such sources as Professional Film Tools at <http://shop.store.yahoo.com/cinemasupplies/chromkeyfab.html> or complete virtual sets can be obtained from Virtual Set Works <http://www.virtualsetworks.com/>.

If a library media specialist or teacher chooses to paint his own wall for a screen, the location should be the first consideration. Will all light from the sun, street lamps, or other external sources be completely blocked? Chroma Keying is not difficult, but its success depends on the correct color and strength of light. A person can buy the most saturated Chroma Green paint that Rosco sells, but primer and three coats of the cheapest flat primary green paint from Sherwin Williams will work as well.

After preparing the Chroma Key background, the next consideration is the clothing of the talent. It is important that the subject does not wear the same color clothing as the color of the background or the subject's dress or shirt will magically disappear. It is also critical to keep the lines on the subject simple and smooth, because fine, detailed lines do not key well. When videotaping a shot that will later be Chroma Keyed, it is best to try to limit the subject's movements. A quickly moving subject carries with it a motion blur where the subject and key background blend.

Finalizing and Rendering a Video

As with all computer projects, it is important to save the project from time to time so that the work will not be lost because of computer trouble. Saving a video project does not render the movie or create a file that can play on a VCR. It merely saves the file in the native format of the video-editing software so it can be worked on later.

Each time a component is added to a video project, the creator may want to preview the entire result. Are the transitions too fast? Does the text just sit there and get boring? To know what has been created thus far, the creator will have to preview the project. If the creator simply presses play in the video editor at this time, probably only the most recent video clip will be seen without the added special effects, transitions, and text. Before an edited video can be played back to tape, the computer must "render" or "make" the finished movie as a single continuous file. Once this new file is created, the video can be played back anytime with the click of a mouse. Often the track audio cannot be heard until the track has finished rendering.

Some video-editing software contains dual preview monitors. These virtual monitors enable the user to preview individual video files as well as the entire timeline. Users can operate in dual virtual monitor mode using one virtual monitor, the source monitor for clip previews, and the program monitor to preview the entire timeline of the movie.

One misunderstood aspect of digital video editing is *rendering*. Before starting to render, make sure there is enough disk space to create the finished movie. The more titles, effects, and filters used, the more megabytes the finished file will be. The rendering process requires a lot of computer power and time so more RAM and a faster processor will make a big difference. Rendering can take 10 to 20 times as long as the total time of the finished movie, therefore rendering times of several hours are common.

Once everything is rendered, the video is ready to output. Video creators can output their movie in multiple formats. An understanding of the different distribution formats (covered in Chapter Six) will help the video creator determine the best settings for each output format. For archival purposes, outputting back to a digital video tape is still the best quality option available.

Summary:

Digital video editing can be considered as cheating time and changing reality. With the right software, students can learn to cut, delete, insert, and rearrange video clips along with adding effective transitions between the clips. Multiple layers of digital video and digital audio can be combined into a complex mosaic of sight and sound. Digital video editing opens a form of self-expression that was only recently available to the professionals.

Chapter

Evaluating Student Videos

N o project is complete without evaluation and feedback. Even before a student begins an assigned video, she needs to be aware of the expectations of what consists of a good video. Teachers can express these expectations in a variety of formats from a checklist to a rubric, but the basic evaluation guidelines remain the same.

The most important criteria to pass on to the students are—does the video fulfill the goals and objectives the creator intended? While details may evolve during the production of the video, the basic objectives should be determined and clearly stated in the pre-planning stage of development.

Similar to an oral or print report, detailed and accurate research must be the cornerstone of a video project and should be evaluated accordingly. Research questions need to be accurately recorded and interpreted either on traditional note cards or in a digital format. Relevant pro and con arguments with supporting facts need to be identified and documented, and the sources need to be cited in proper MLA or APA format. Even though all the source of the research may not be provided to the viewer, it needs to be available if any questions arise as to the creditability and authenticity of any given fact or point-of-view.

Throughout the production process, the teacher needs to monitor the development of the student's storyboard. Items in a detailed storyboard will include descriptions of effective transitions, special effects, sound, and title tracks. In evaluating title tracks, consideration needs to be given to the text color, size, type of font, background color, and the placement and size of graphics. The storyboard needs to include notes concerning the proposed dialog or narration. To avoid confusion, the sketches or frames within a storyboard need to be numbered, and in a logical sequence.

In evaluating student videos, the most weight needs to be given to the video content and organization. The content needs to include a clear statement of purpose and be creative, compelling, and clearly presented in a logical order. A rich variety of supporting information in a video will contribute to the understanding of the main idea of the video project.

Special emphasis needs to be placed on the introduction of a video. The introduction needs to be compelling and provide motivating content that hooks the viewer from the beginning and keeps the audience's attention throughout the video.

While similarities between print, oral, or video presentations abound, the evaluation of the production quality of a video provides a uniqueness of that particular media expression. In the evaluation of the continuity and editing of a video production, it needs to be determined that only high quality shots are included in the final video and the video moves smoothly from shot to shot. The transitions between clips need to assist in communicating the main idea and smooth the flow seamlessly from one scene to the next. All digital effects must be used appropriately for emphasis.

In evaluating the audio and voice editing, the teacher must determine if the audio is clear and effectively assists in communicating the main idea. Did the students communicate ideas with enthusiasm, proper voice projection, appropriate language, and clear delivery? Is the background audio kept in balance and not overpower the primary audio?

Consideration must also be given to the color scheme used in a video. The backgrounds and clothing need to be selected to suit the mood of the video. All scenes must have sufficient lighting for viewers to easily see the action and additional lighting used when necessary to eliminate shadows and glares.

When evaluating camera techniques, teachers must determine that all shots are clearly focused and well framed to be considered an excellent project. The video must be steady with few pans and zooms. Close-ups must only be used to focus attention and the video must show evidence of good composition such as ratio of image to frame, line of gaze, pan/tilts, movements, and perspectives. Motion scenes must be planned and purposeful, adding impact to the story line. "Talking heads" scenes are used only when crucial to telling the story.

It is important that the special effects in the video add to the mood and style of the video and are not used too extensively and distract from the impact of the video. The graphics, sound, and animation must be used to assist in presenting an overall theme that appeals to the audience and enhances the concepts with a high impact message. All multimedia elements should work together, demonstrate excellent synthesis, and reinforce key points during the presentation in order to be considered a work of excellence. Graphic images must be clear with proper size and resolution. Copyrighted information for photos, graphics, and music must be clearly identified by source and nature of permission to reproduce.

The pace and timing of a video must be taken into consideration when evaluating student work. Do all the video clips fit the storyline? Is each clip long enough to make a clear point and capture the audience's attention without belaboring a point? A video clip should not include any slack time. It should be determined that "three beat" timing is evident in which there are three actions per clip or three clips per event.

Video production is rarely a one-person task, but the work of a team of students, each with different responsibilities. Therefore, each video crew needs to provide evidence that each group member helped one another, shared ideas, developed, and evaluated their finished product. Each individual must demonstrate his efforts to capitalize on strengths of other team members.

Summary:

With detailed instruction and evaluation of video production, students will learn to use and improve their 21st century technology skills. With these new skills, students will be able to apply higher order thinking skills, improve their decision-making, and increase their creative thinking and collaboration skills. Through evaluating their video productions, students will increase their visual literacy while broadening their media literacy in understanding the world around them.

Chapter 12

Organizing a

School TV News Show

Class versus Video Club

With the increase of closed circuit TVs in schools, student-produced news shows are becoming more and more common. Schools that subscribe to Channel One News can utilize their equipment to project their school news throughout the building. Often, local cable companies will wire a school for closed circuit for little or no cost.

There are two approaches to producing school news shows. The "run in, shoot, and produce it" approach, which relies on a group of students showing up in the media center or TV studio consistently at a designated time. The "run in, shoot, and produce it" approach accomplishes the goal of producing a news show and projecting the school news throughout the school, but it rarely leaves time for video instruction or the development of media skills. Producing a news show with this method is stressful for both students and the media specialist since there is little room for error, and none for growth.

If the "run in, shoot, and produce it" approach is all that can be worked into the school schedule, library media specialists need to squeeze in time for instruction, practice, and critique from an overcrowded schedule. A few minutes several times a week is necessary to teach and demonstrate techniques, evaluate, and provide feedback for the production crew.

To evaluate the school news show and decide if the show educates students and serves the school, certain questions need to be considered. Does the news show have useful content for students and teachers? Are students learning media production skills while working on the news show? Are the major features of the equipment being utilized? Is the school-news production time overly stressful? If the answers to the above questions are yes, it may be time to talk with the administration about adopting the second method of school-news production. This method includes teaching a media class and incorporating the skills learned in the class into the school news show.

The benefits of changing from the "run in, shoot, and produce it" approach to a media production class would include the teaching of media skills, verbal skills, and teamwork that would help build self-esteem. A media class would put more focus on student achievement. Instead of just reading the list of student achievers, a media class will have time to provide a digital image or a videotaped segment about the student achievers. With time for media instruction, meaningful segments can be developed in a purposeful manner. The lunch menu can be replaced with an interview with the cafeteria manager explaining the importance of good nutrition. The weather report can become a full-weekend forecast with students researching on the Internet and writing a script.

Even though a daily period for broadcasting is scheduled, classroom teachers can become preoccupied and forget to turn on their televisions for the news show. The first week or two of the school year, it would be advisable to announce over the intercom a minute or two before playing the tape or broadcasting the show.

One of the first decisions a media specialist will make is whether to broadcast live or to prerecord a show for later broadcast. Most community television news shows are done as live broadcasts, but students in a learning environment do not usually possess the maturity of professional newscasters. Taping a program and broadcasting later in the day eliminates many problems that can occur during live broadcasts.

Weekly or monthly broadcasts are less difficult to schedule. These shows are generally longer than the daily broadcasts and need to be scheduled accordingly.

Setting

The type of news show will in part determine the setting. Will it be a serious journalistic approach or a humorous and entertaining broadcast? A news-magazine set differs from the typical anchor-desk format in that the news anchors are not seated behind a formal news-anchor desk. In a news-magazine format, the anchors may use chairs or stools or may even be standing in a more casual and relaxed 'living room' style setting.

Content Format

What kind of information will be included in each show? Will Monday's show differ from Thursday's? Maintaining a consistent show format helps both the production crew and the viewer. For example, each day the format for a community television news show stays the same, while the content changes daily. The basic format includes major news event, national news, local news, weather, and sports in that order. In planning the content of a news show, start simple and build as students gain experience with the equipment and techniques.

Another issue to be considered is who will present the announcements on air. Will any administrators be involved in the daily broadcasts? How many anchors will host the show? Will the opening shot include both anchors and a welcome or just a one-time shot of a single anchor? How many cameras will be used to record the show and what angles will each one be using?

Music can add interest and attract the viewers' attention. If canned music is used as an introduction, when students hear the familiar music, they know what to expect. As soon as the music introduction ends, usually the camera moves to the co-anchors who give a personal welcome and introduce themselves. An anchor then introduces the first story along with all the lead-ins to every segment.

Finally, how will the show end? Will there be ending graphics, music, and rolling credits, or a simple "That's our show for today—see you tomorrow" from the anchors?

Student Personnel

Many media specialists prefer to select a production team from student applications with teacher recommendations. Letting only the gifted and talented class produce the news show is not a fair way of distributing the opportunities for learning media skills and techniques. Many students with learning challenges excel in visual and media literacy and can gain a great deal from participating in a school news show.

As the "director" of a student-produced news program, it is a good idea for the media specialist or sponsoring teacher to create a manual of student-produced news policies and procedures. There is no need to write pages and pages of policies and procedures, but it is a good idea to have in place the program goals, the tone of the program preferred, and the types of activities that are to be included in the show.

An important issue to cover in the student-produced news manual is guidelines for students to avoid libel. Students need help in understanding the implications of the First Amendment and their rights and responsibilities. Through instruction, students will see what constitutes libel and learn to balance their responsibility to inform their viewers against their responsibility to protect the subjects of their reporting.

Before selecting the students that will become the production team, it is important to identify the jobs or positions needed. NEVER have more students than jobs. ("Idle hands …")

The more sophisticated the show, the more students are needed to fill the positions. Common positions include producer, technical director, audio technician, graphics technician, camera operator, videotape operator, teleprompter operator, talent, and reporter.

Guidelines for Students in Front of a Camera

- On-camera talents need to maintain an open posture with their backs straight; arms, legs, and feet relaxed and uncrossed. Slouching creates an image of disinterest.

- On-camera talents should lean forward. Leaning slightly forward demonstrates interest while leaning backward demonstrates rejection or aloofness.

- On-camera talents should try to mirror what the interviewee is doing. They need to be conscious of the guest's breathing and the pace at which she is talking. Is it fast or slow?

- On-camera talents need to look at the camera frequently. Learning how to read ahead on the script is an important skill for the student to master.

- On-camera talents should maintain direct eye contact. Direct eye contact is a compliment to most people and builds their trust.

- On-camera talents must keep going even when a mistake is made. If the section has to be redone, the director or producer will make that decision.

- On-camera talents need to read as if they are telling a story so the inflection will be their own, not a dry monotone.

- On-camera talents should develop an on-screen personality. Few professional broadcasters act the same way in front of a camera as they do in real life.

Tips for Preparing an Interview

The interview is an easy segment of the newscast to produce. The script requirements are minor. The on-camera talent introduces the segment. The newscast cuts to the interview, after which the interviewer sends it back to the studio for a wrap-up or conclusion.

After the primary question has been answered, the interviewer should anticipate how the interview might proceed and be prepared should it take some unexpected turn. To avoid uncomfortable pauses, the interviewer must avoid questions that elicit simple yes and no answers whenever possible and always have more questions to ask than will be needed. The interviewer should be prepared to branch away from the prepared topic if the interview begins going in a particularly interesting direction. When preparing questions, the interviewer might ask herself, "How do I expect the interviewee to answer my question? What will I do if the answer comes back differently than I expected?"

Preparing Audio to be Used in a Newcast

- During an interview for broadcast, be sure and use whole sentences. It is best to wait five to seven seconds before speaking in case the interviewee has something more to say.

- The cameraperson needs to hear what the camera hears and use an earphone plugged into the camera instead of relying strictly on her ears.

- The audio technicians should always do a sound check. This simple, yet annoying check helps the video gauge how the on-screen talent will sound and how well the microphone picks up the voice.

- During the actual shot, the audio technicians should try to anticipate moments when the speaker speaks softly or when the speaker shouts so that even audio levels can be maintained.

- Always keep plenty of backup batteries for the microphones on hand.

Caring for Equipment

Care of audio/video equipment is a vital skill to be taught to the school television news-show crew. As students become comfortable with the equipment they will gain pride and self-respect for having the privilege of being trusted with expensive equipment.

Guidelines for Care of the Camcorder

- Handle the equipment only when necessary.
- Be careful where the camera is set, so that it will not be knocked off the table.
- Avoid jarring and bumping.
- Use a tripod when possible.
- Avoid touching the lens or viewfinder as the glass gets oily and is hard to keep clean.
- Replace the lens cover and remove tapes and batteries after each use.
- Avoid temperature extremes and condensation.

Television Production and the School Media Program

Because many students are proficient with multimedia presentations and surfing the Internet, some educators are beginning to question whether school television is still necessary in schools. School video production has benefits that should not be overlooked. The basics of video production can be learned quickly and after 15 minutes of instruction, a team of students can videotape a good interview or mini-documentary. Graphics, title, and audio dubbing are skills that can quickly be learned and transferred to multimedia production. In communicating an idea, seeing a human face on the screen, as opposed to a rotating screen, adds greater impact to the message.

Another question media specialists or media instructors face is the amount of time to commit to school video production. The only correct answer is whatever is reasonable and comfortable for the individual media specialist in her particular school environment. Problems can develop when classes or individual students are overlooked in preference to the video production. As in all programs in a school, balance is the key. The main questions to consider; Is the school newscast adding to the communications within the school? Are the video production crews gaining valuable skills and self-confidence while preparing their school newscasts? Is the school news show increasing the media and visual literacy within the school? Does the school news show meet technology standards and support the mission of the school?

Summary:

Nothing can replace the advantage of having a media production class, but if it is not possible to have a separate class, a creative teacher or media specialist can still develop media skills in his students by organizing a video club. Preparing a school news show and attending before- and after-school meetings can provide students with a format and time to learn on-camera skills, audio and video editing skills, care of equipment, and content planning. Having control of their own school news helps both the student participants and the viewers broaden their interest and understanding of local and national news and prepares them to stay informed of current events and face a fast changing world.

 *Works Cited* _____

Adobe Audition 1.5. Adobe Systems, Inc. 13 July 2004
    <http://www.adobe.com/products/audition/>.

Adobe Premiere Pro 1.5. Adobe Systems, Inc. 13 July 2004
    <http://store.adobe.com/products/premiere/>.

American Memory for Historical Collections of the National Digital Library. Library of
    Congress. 13 July 2004 <http://memory.loc.gov>.

Audacity. 13 July 2004 <http://audacity.sourceforge.net/>.

Bell, Ann. *Creating Computer Video in the Classroom.* University of Wisconsin—Stout. 13
    July 2004 <http://www.uwstout.edu/soe/profdev/video/>.

Blake, Bonnie, and Doug Sahlin. *50 Fast Digital Video Techniques.* Hoboken, NJ: Wiley, 2003.

Children's Internet Protection Act Requirements. Universal Service Administrative
    Company. 13 July 2004 <http://www.sl.universalservice.org/reference/CIPA.asp>.

Clipart.com. 13 July 2004 <http://clipart.com>.

Copyright Clearance Center. 13 July 2004 <http://www.copyright.com/>.

Copyright Kids. The Copyright Society of the U.S.A. 13 July 2004
    <http://www.copyrightkids.org>.

Create Home Movies with Windows Movie Maker. Microsoft Corp. 13 July 2004
    <http://www.microsoft.com/windowsxp/using/moviemaker/default.mspx>.

Curchy, Christopher, and Keith Kyker. *Educator's Survival Guide for Television Production
    and Activities.* Westport, CT.: Libraries Unlimited, 2003.
    . *Educator's Survival Guide to TV Production and Setup.* Englewood: Libraries
    Unlimited, 1998.
    . *Television Production: A Classroom Approach.* Englewood: Libraries Unlimited, 1993.

Cybercollege.com. CyberColl. Internet Campus. 13 July 2004
    <http://www.cybercollege.com/>.

Digital Licensing. Harry Fox Agency, Inc. 13 July 2004
    <http://www.harryfox.com/digital.html>.

Doucette, Martin. *Digital Video for Dummies.* Forest City, CA: IDE, 2001.

Explore iLive. Apple Computer, Inc. 13 July 2004 <http://www.apple.com/ilife/>.

Federal Trade Commission. *Children's Online Privacy Protection Act.* 13 July 2004
    <http://www.ftc.gov/ogc/coppa1.htm>.

Final Cut Pro HD. Apple Computers, Inc. 13 July 2004
    <http://www.apple.com/finalcutpro/>.

"Five Key Questions." *MediaLit Kit.* Center for Media Literacy. 13 July 2004
    <http://www.medialit.org/reading_room/pdf/04KeyQuestionsBW.pdf>.

Flynn, Deras. *TechTV's Guide to Creating Digital Video like a Pro.* Indianapolis: Que, 2002.

Gold Wave Digital Audio Editor. GoldWave, Inc. 13 July 2004 <http://www.goldwave.ca/>.

Gorham, Ramona, and Virgina Wallace. *School News Shows: Video Production with a Focus*. Worthington, OH: Linworth, 1996.

Greenword, Daniel R. *Action! In the Classroom*. Landham, MD.: Scarecrow, 2003.

"Information Literacy Standards for Student Learning." *Information Power: Building Partnerships for Learning*. Chicago: ALA, 1998. 844. Rpt. in *Information Literacy Standards for Student Learning*.

Inspiration Software. Inspiration Software, Inc. 13 July 2004 <http://www.inspiration.com/home.cfm>.

ISTE National Educational Technology Standards (NETS) and Performance Indicators for Teachers. 2000. International Society for Technology in Education. 13 July 2004 <http://cnets.iste.org/teachers/pdf/page09.pdf>.

Kenny, Robert. *Teaching TV Production in a Digital World*. Englewood: Libraries Unlimited, 2001.

Kids' Vid. High Plains Regional Technology in Education Consortium. 13 July 2004 <http://kidsvid.hprtec.org/>.

Limitations on Exclusive Rights: Fair Use. 19 Oct. 1976 <http://www4.law.cornell.edu/uscode/17/107.html>.

Maguire, James, and Jim Louderback. *TechTV's Secrets of the Digital Studio: Insider's Guide to Destop Recording*. Indianapolis: QUE, 2002.

McConnell, Terry, and Harry W. Sprouse. *Video Production for School Library Media Specialist*. Worthington, OH: Linworth, 2000.

Microphones University. DPA Microphones A/S. 13 July 2004 <http://www.dpamicrophones.com/>.

"Miles Guide for 21st Century Skills." *Learning for the 21st Century*. 21st Century Skills Organization. Partnership for 21st Century Skills. Washington, D.C. 13 July 2004 <http://www.21stcenturyskills.org/downloads/P21_Report.pdf>.

MIRA Stock Photography Agency of the Creative Eye. Creative Eye. 13 July 2004 <http://mira.com/>.

Motion Picture Licensing Corp. 13 July 2004 <http://www.mplc.com/index2.htm>.

Pics4Learning. Partners in Education and Orange County Public Schools. 13 July 2004 <http://www.pics4learning.com>.

Pinnacle Studio AV/DV 9. Pinnacle Systems. 13 July 2004 <http://www.pinnaclesys.com/ProductPage_n.asp?Product_ID=2050&Langue_ID=7>.

Public Domain Music. Haven Sound, Inc. 13 July 2004 <http://www.pdinfo.com>.

Rubin, Michael. *The Little Digital Video Book*. Berkeley: Peachpit, 2002.

Sammons, Martha C. *Multimedia Presentations on the Go*. Englewood: Libraries Unlimited, 1996.

SongFile.com. Harry Fox, Agency. 13 July 2004 <http://www.songfile.com/>.

Steward, Winston. *Digital Video Sollutions*. Cincinnati: Muska & Lipman, 2002.

Storyboard Pro Software. Atomic Learning, Inc. 13 July 2004 <http://www.atomiclearning.com/storyboardpro>.

"Students Who Are Visually Literate." *21st Century Skills*. North Central Regional Educational Laboratory. 13 July 2004 <http://www.ncrel.org/engauge/skills/vislit.htm>.

"Teacher's/Leader's Orientation Guide." *MediaLit Kit*. 2002. Center for Media Literacy. 13 July 2004 <http://www.medialit.org/bp_mlk.html>.

Technology Foundation Standards for All Students. 2004. International Society for Technology in Education. 13 July 2004 <http://cnets.iste.org/students/s_stands.html>.

The New iMovie. Apple Computer, Inc. 13 July 2004 <http://www.apple.com/ilife/imovie/>.

Theodosakis, Nikos. *The Director in the Classroom: How Filmmaking Inspires Learning*. San Diego: Tech4Learning, 2001.

Thurrott, Paul. *Great Digital Media with Windows XP*. New York: Hungry Minds, 2001.

ULead MediaStudio Pro. ULead Systems. 13 July 2004 <http://www.ulead.com/msp/>.

United States Copyright Office. *Reproduction of Copyrighted Works by Educators and Librarians*. 13 July 2004 <http://www.copyright.gov/circs/circ21.pdf>.

U.S. Copyright Office. *The Digital Millenium Copyright Act of 1998*. 13 July 2004 <http://www.copyright.gov/legislation/dmca.pdf>.

Vandervelde, Joan. "A+ Rubric." *Video Project Rubric*. University of Wisconsin—Stout. 13 July 2004 <http://www.uwstout.edu/soe/profdev/videorubric.html>.

"What a Microphone Does." *A Brief Guide to Microphones*. Audio-Technia U.S., Inc., 13 July 2004 <http://www.audiotechnia.com/using/mphones/guide/micdoes.html>.

"What Is Visual Literacy?" *International Visual Literacy Association*. 13 July 2004 <http://www.ivla.org/org_what_vis_lit.htm>.

Waggoner, Ben, *Compression for Great Digital Video*. Lawrence, KS: CMP, 2002.

York, Matt, ed. *The Computer Videomaker Handbook*. Boston: Focal, 2001.

Youth Media Distribution Tool Kit. Youth Media Distribution. 13 July 2004 <http://www.ymdi.org/toolkit/archives/000491.php>.

A/B rolls. Video editing technique of taking video snippets from deck or track "A" and merging them with snippets from deck or track "B".

Acceptable Use Policy (AUP). Guidelines for the appropriate use of computer networks. A written agreement in the form of guidelines, signed by students, their parents, and their teachers, outlining the terms and conditions of Internet use, rules of online behavior, and access privileges.

Acoustics. The total effect of sound, especially as produced in an enclosed space.

Adapter. A device used to affect operative compatibility between different parts of one or more pieces of apparatus.

Alternating current (AC). An electric current that periodically changes or reverses its direction of flow. In the US most household current is AC at 60 cycles per second.

American Wire Gauge (AWG). A U.S. standard set of non-ferrous wire conductor sizes. Typical household wiring is AWG number 12 or 14. Telephone wire is usually 22, 24, or 26. The higher the gauge number, the smaller the diameter and the thinner the wire. Thicker wire is better for long distances due to its lower resistance per unit length.

Ambient sound (ambience). Natural background audio representative of given recording environment.

Amplitude. The maximum absolute value reached by a voltage or current waveform.

Analog. An electrical signal directly generated from a stimulus of a circuit or device having an output that is proportional to the input signal.

Audio channel. Audio channels are the number of more or less independent audio streams. Mono sound uses one audio channel, stereo uses two audio channels.

Back light. Illumination from behind. Creates a sense of depth by separating foreground subject from background area.

Background lights. Illuminates the background area and adds depth and separation between scene elements. (A back light is designed to light up *the back of subjects* and a background light is designed to light up *the front of backgrounds*.)

Bandwidth. A data transmission rate; the maximum amount of information (bits/second) that can be transmitted along a channel.

Barn door. Black metal flaps that fit around a light to keep the light from going where you don't want it to go.

Bit rate. (or "bitrate") Ratio of the number of bits per second that are transferred between devices in a specified amount of time. Bit rate is the same as data rate, data transfer rate, and bit time.

Bitmap. Method of storing information that maps an image pixel, bit by bit. A bitmap is characterized by the width and height of the image in pixels and the number of bits per pixel, which determines the number of shades of gray, or colors it can represent.

BNC connector. A video connector for coaxial cable characterize by a single shaft enclosed by a twist-lock mechanism.

Boom. Extension arm used to suspend a microphone or camera over sound or subject being recorded.

Capture. A procedure performed by a computer's capture card to digitize material from a video/audio source and store it on the computer's hard drive.

Capture card. Computer card that converts video from a camcorder into video in a computer.

Cardioid. Another name for the unidirectional microphone heart-shaped pick-up pattern.

CD-R. Compact Disc-Recordable. A recordable version of a standard CD-ROM disc.

Charge coupled device (CCD). Collects visual images in a camera and converts the image into either an analog or a digital signal.

Chroma Key. Overlaying one video signal over another. Areas of the overlay are a specific color (such as chroma blue or green). The chroma color is made transparent.

Chrominance. The part of a video signal pertaining to hue and saturation.

Close-up. Tightly framed camera shot in which the principal subject is viewed at close range, appearing relatively large and dominant on screen.

Coaxial cable. A cable consisting of a conducting outer metal tube enclosing and insulated from a central conducting core. Used for high-frequency transmission of telephone, telegraph, and television signals.

Codec (compressor/decompressor). A method used to compress and decompress images and sound data so that files are smaller and easier for a computer to manage.

Color temperature. A way of standardizing the interpretation of color among various recording and playback devices. Measured in degrees Kelvin.

Composite video. Single video signal combining luminance and chrominance signals through an encoding process, including image's separate RGB (red, green, blue) elements and sync information.

Composition. Visual makeup of a video picture, including such variables as balance, framing, field of view, texture—all aesthetic considerations.

Compression. The coding of data to save storage space or transmission time. Compressed data must be decompressed before it can be used.

Condenser microphone. A microphone with built-in amplifier. Requires battery or external power source.

CPU (central processing unit). The primary intelligence chip of a computer system. The term is often used to refer to the entire housing of a computer.

Cutaways. Shot of other than the principal action (but peripherally related). Frequently used as transitional footage or to avoid a jump cut.

Data rate. The amount of data a mass storage medium (such as a hard disk) saves and plays back per second. Also, the amount of data in one second of a video sequence.

Decibels (dB). The unit of measure for sound pressure level (loudness).

Diaphragm. A thin disk, especially in a microphone or telephone receiver, that vibrates in response to sound waves to produce electric signals, or that vibrates in response to electric signals to produce sound waves.

Digital zoom. A feature found in some camcorders that electronically increases the lens zoom capability by selecting the center of the image and enlarging it digitally.

Digital8. A format of digital camcorders that use 8mm or Hi-8 tapes for storage.

Digitizer. Device that imports and converts analog video images into digital information for hard drive-based editing.

Distortion. An undesired change in the waveform of a signal.

Directional microphone. Capable of receiving or sending signals in one direction only.

DivX. A digital video codec created by DivXNetworks, Inc.

Dolby Surround Sound. Dolby Digital is the de facto surround sound standard in home and movie theaters today.

Dolly. (v) A forward/backward rolling movement of the camera on top of the tripod dolly. (n) A set of casters attached to the legs of a tripod to allow the tripod to roll.

DV bridge. A digital video pass-through device.

Dynamic microphone. Works much like a loudspeaker in reverse, employing a simple diaphragm, magnet, and wire coil to convert sound waves into an electrical signal.

Equalizer. A tone control system designed to compensate for frequency distortion in audio systems.

Feedback. Echo effect at low levels, howl or piercing squeal at extremes, from audio signal being fed back to itself.

Field of view. Extent of a shot that is visible through a particular lens.

Fill light. A light that partially (but not entirely) fills in the shadows created by the horizontal and vertical angles of the key light.

Filter. Transparent or semi-transparent material mounted at the front of a camcorder lens to change light passing through. Manipulates colors and image patterns, often for special effect purposes.

Firewire (IEEE 1394 or i.LINK). A high-speed bus that is used, among other things, to connect digital camcorders to computers.

Font. A specific size and style of type within a type family.

Frame. One complete image. In NTSC video a frame is composed of two fields, 1/30th of a second.

Frame rate. Number of video frames per second. NTSC is 30 frames per second.

Frequency. Number of vibrations produced by a signal or sound, usually expressed as cycles per second, or hertz (Hz). Determines the pitch of a sound.

Gif (Graphics Interchange Format). A bit-mapped graphics file format used by the World Wide Web.

H.263. A video compression (coding) standard, published by the International Telecommunications Union (ITU), for video-conferencing and video-telephony applications.

Hertz (Hz). A unit of electrical vibrations consisting of one cycle of frequency per second.

Hi-8 (high-band 8mm). Improved version of 8mm videotape format characterized by higher luminance resolution for a sharper picture.

IEEE 1394 (Firewire). A connecting device used to connect digital video camcorders to personal computers and nonlinear digital editing systems. The IEEE 1394 signal carries audio and video tracks and is capable of speeds up to 400 megabytes per second. (IEEE is the Institute of Electrical and Electronic Engineers.)

In loco parentis. In the position or place of a parent.

Indeo. A codec (compression/decompression technology) for digital video developed by Intel Corporation.

Jack. Any female socket or receptacle, usually on the backside of video and audio equipment; accepts plug for circuit connection.

JPEG (Joint Photographic Experts Group). A lossy compression technique for color images.

Jump cut. Unnatural, abrupt switch to/from shots identical in subject but slightly different in screen location.

Kelvin scale (K). Measurement of the temperature of light in color recording.

Keyframe. A single frame of digital content that the compressor examines independent of the frames that precede and follow it, which stores all of the data needed to display that frame.

Key light. Principal illumination source on a subject or scene normally positioned slightly off center and angled to set the directions of shadow in a scene.

KiloHertz (KHz). One thousand hertz or cycles per second of frequency.

Lavaliere microphone. A very small microphone that clips on to a person's clothing.

Linear editing. Tape-based editing. Called linear because scenes are laid in a line along the tape.

Long shot. Camera view of a subject or scene, usually from a distance, showing a broad perspective.

Lossy compression. A term describing a data compression algorithm, which actually reduces the amount of information in the data, rather than just the number of bits used to represent that information. The lost information is removed because it is subjectively less important to the quality of an image or sound.

Lossless compression. Data compression technique in which no data is lost. For most types of data, lossless compression techniques can reduce the space needed by only about 50 percent.

Luminance. The part of a video image signal carrying brightness information.

Masks. A filter that selectively includes or excludes certain values.

Media Access Generator (MAGpie). An authoring tool that creates captions and audio descriptions for rich media.

Medium shot. A camera shot that shows the entire head of a human subject and cuts off the human body at the waist.

MegaHertz (MHz). One million cycles per second of frequency.

MIDI (Musical Instrument Digital Interface). A standard means of sending digitally encoded music information between electronic devices, such as between a synthesizer and a computer.

MiniDV (minidigital video). A miniaturized digital video format.

Monotone. Sameness or dull repetition in sound, style, manner, or color.

MP3. (MPEG-1 Audio Layer-3) A digital audio format for compressing sound into a very small computer file, while preserving the original level of quality.

MPEG (Motion Picture Experts Group). Defines standards for compressing moving images. Also, a kind of compression that reduces the size and bandwidth of a video signal.

MPEG-1. Format for compressed video, optimized for CD-ROM.

MPEG-2. Digital video compression used in DVDs and DSS satellite TV systems.

Nonlinear digital video editing. Post-production work using audio and video elements saved as digital files on a computer hard drive or some other storage device.

NTSC (National Television System Committee). NTSC is the video signal used in televisions, VCRs, and videotapes in the United States, Japan, and Canada.

Neutral density filter. A piece of glass that fits over the lens of a camcorder used for outdoor shooting on bright sunny days.

Omni-directional microphone. Absorbs sounds from all directions.

Optical zoom. Uses the optics (lens) of the camera to bring the subject closer.

PAL (phase alternate line). 625-line 50-field-per-second television signal standard used in Europe and South America. Incompatible with NTSC.

Panning. The horizontal turning of a camera.

PCI slots. A standard for connecting peripherals to a personal computer.

Plug. The end of the cable that fits into a jack on a piece of video, audio, or computer equipment.

Point-of-view (POV) shot. Shot perspective whereby the camera assumes the subject's view and the viewers see what the subject sees.

Polarizing filter. Mounts at the front of the camcorder lens and thwarts undesirable glare and reflection.

Pressure zone microphone. Omni-directional microphone placed in the center of a room used to record a conversation between people.

QuickTime. Computer system software that defines a format for video and audio data, so different applications can open and play synchronized sound and movie files.

RCA connection. Standard connection for direct audio/video inputs/outputs.

Reflector. Lighting accessory helpful for bouncing light onto a subject as well as filling in shadows.

Rendering. The processing a computer undertakes when creating an applied effect, transition, or composite.

Resolution. Amount of picture detail reproduced by a video system, influenced by a camera's pickup, lens, internal optics, recording medium, and playback monitor.

Retensioning. The process where a tape is unspooled onto a take-up reel and then rewound at a controlled tension and speed.

RF (radio frequency). Combination of audio and video signals coded as a channel number, necessary for television broadcasts as well as some closed-circuit distribution.

RF converter. Device that converts audio and video signals into a combined RF signal suitable for reception by a standard TV.

RGB (red, green, blue). Video signal transmission system that differentiates and processes all color information in separate red, green, and blue components—primary colors of light—for optimum image quality. Also defines type of color monitor.

Ripping. Digitally extracting audio or video tracks from a CD or DVD so they can be stored as a file on a computer.

Rule of thirds. Composition theory based on the screen being divided into thirds vertically and horizontally and the placement of important elements along those lines.

SP/DIF (Sony/Philips Digital Interface). A standard audio file transfer format that allows the transfer of digital audio signals from one device to another without having to be converted first to an analog.

Sample rate. The rate at which samples of an analog signal are taken in order to be converted into digital form. Typically expressed in samples per second, or hertz (Hz).

Sans serif font. A category of typefaces that do not use serifs, small lines at the ends of characters. Sans serif fonts are more difficult to read and are used most often for short text components such as headlines or captions.

Scan converter. An electronic device that changes the scan rate of a video signal. A scan converter provides the means for a computer image to be recorded on videotape or displayed on a standard video monitor or projector.

Scrub. The action with a video-editing program that causes the video to move frame by frame.

Serif font. A small decorative line added as embellishment to the basic form of a character.

Shotgun microphone. A unidirectional microphone similar to a zoom microphone used to pick up sound in areas a person cannot go.

Sibilants. A hissing sound like that of (s) or (sh).

Storyboard. A plan for the shooting of a scene or scenes for a video. Also, a plan for the ordering of individual segments during editing.

Super-8. Super 8mm film format was developed by Kodak in 1965 to replace regular 8mm.

S-VHS. A video format that uses VHS-sized cassettes and a 1/2 inch S-VHS tape and produces a signal with more than 400 lines of resolution.

S-video. Also known as Y/C video, signal type employed with Hi-8 and S-VHS video formats. Transmits chrominance and luminance portions separately via multiple wires.

Telephoto lens. Camera lens with long focal length, narrow horizontal field of view that captures magnified, close-up images from considerable distance.

Three-point lighting. Basic lighting approach employing key, back, and fill lights to illuminate subject with sense of depth and texture.

TIFF (tagged image file format). A file format used for still-image bitmaps, stored in tagged fields.

Timeline. A workspace within a video-editing program in which the video and audio clips are represented on the computer screen by bars proportional to the length of the clip.

Transition. A video scene that links two adjoining scenes.

Transmitter. An electronic device that generates and amplifies a carrier wave, modulates it with a meaningful signal derived from speech or other sources, and radiates the resulting signal from an antenna.

Tripod. A mounting device for a camera that has three legs. Helps the camera operator achieve a steady camera shot.

Unidirectional microphone. Contains a highly selective pickup pattern, rejects sound coming from behind while absorbing that from in front.

VCD (video compact disk). A storage format used for video or film distribution.

VHS (video home system). Predominant half-inch videotape format.

VHS-C (VHS compact). Scaled-down version of VHS using miniature cassettes compatible with full-size VHS equipment through use of an adapter.

Video compositing. The process of merging two videos (or a single video and still image) to display one combined video. Compositing is also called "overlaying", as in overlaying one video over another, and "blue screen" or "green screen", which are specific compositing techniques used to combine two videos.

Voice over (VO). Narration accompanying picture, heard above background sound or music.

VU meter. Volume unit on an audio mixer.

White balance. To adjust the camera's color response to existing light.

Wide-angle lens. Camera lens with short focal length and broad horizontal field of view. Opposite of telephoto lens. Provides viewer perspective and reinforces perception of depth.

Windscreens. Sponge-like microphone shield which thwarts undesirable noise from wind and rapid mike movement.

Wireless/RF microphone. A microphone with no cables connected to it.

XLR (ground-left-right). Three-pin plug for three-conductor "balanced" audio cable, employed with high-quality microphones, mixers, and other audio equipment.

Zoom microphone. Absorbs sound from 30 feet away.

Index